ZOO WORLD

the journal non/fiction prize

ZOO WORLD

ESSAYS

MARY QUADE

MAD CREEK BOOKS, AN IMPRINT OF
THE OHIO STATE UNIVERSITY PRESS
COLUMBUS

Mad Creek Books, an imprint of The Ohio State University Press.

Library of Congress Cataloging-in-Publication Data
Names: Quade, Mary, author.
Title: Zoo world : essays / Mary Quade.
Description: Columbus : Mad Creek Books, an imprint of The Ohio
    State University Press, [2023] | Includes bibliographical references.
    | Summary: "Melds travel and nature writing to explore humans'
    attempts at redemption for violence they have visited upon the world,
    critically examining relationships with other species and the earth via
    such diverse topics as zoos, insects, ancient churches, tourism, and
    climate change"—Provided by publisher.
Identifiers: LCCN 2023007207 | ISBN 9780814258774 (paperback) |
    ISBN 0814258778 (paperback) | ISBN 9780814282960 (ebook) | ISBN
    0814282962 (ebook)
Subjects: LCSH: Quade, Mary. | Human-animal relationships. | Nature. |
    Travel.
Classification: LCC PS3617.U35 Z66 2023 | DDC 814/.6—dc23/eng/20230417
LC record available at https://lccn.loc.gov/2023007207

Cover design by Lissi Sigillo
Text design by Juliet Williams
Type set in Buckeye Serif

for my students—whose words mean *hope*

contents

hatch

I've been waiting for something that may or may not happen. It's a small something, about the size of an egg. This isn't exactly a comparison, because what I've been waiting for is inside an egg. I'm not a patient person, and spring in northeastern Ohio brings out a special kind of impatience in me, a paradoxical expectation of surprise at the sudden growth around me. It's been just about four weeks. The mallard ducks are patient. They sit and sit, turning the eggs quietly with their bills, pulling out their own feathers to make nests soft. They sit in a kind of liminal state, between life and not life, for weeks. Is this patience or programming?

The week the hens began sitting in earnest, on April 20, the accident occurred in the Gulf Coast. A British Petroleum floating oil derrick called *Deepwater Horizon* drilling into the ocean floor a mile or so below the surface hit a bubble of gas. The rig exploded and, two days later, sank. Now, on the ocean floor, a device called the blowout preventer has burst and leaks oil, uncontrolled, into the sea. There's a hole on the bottom of the sea spewing crude and gas. The story has one clear message: this is bad.

The barn in back of our house isn't a huge barn, like you'd find on a dairy farm, but instead the kind of barn where they kept the horse and buggy in 1906, when the house was built. It has a small storage room and an upstairs loft, presumably for hay. On the ground level, a central set of wide doors faces the house. When we bought the house in 2002, the barn leaned perceptibly, the top half torquing counterclockwise away from the foundation. Years ago, someone had cut through supportive studs to put a standard garage door on the left side of its eastern face. The barn began its slow spin away from true. The people from whom we bought the house offered to knock the structure down.

Instead, my dad and mom came out to visit the July shortly after we moved in, and my dad brought his tools. He attached with cable the torquing front southeast corner of the barn to the base of a steel pole that held a basketball hoop near the back south side of the barn. In this kind of configuration, the pole acting as a ground anchor is called the dead man. It's the thing that won't move. The cable was strung through a winch. Before doing anything else, my dad and my husband, Cris, spent a lot of time staring at the barn, their minds playing out scenarios.

For two weeks after the rig goes down, we're paralyzed by the path of the oil across the water. This is bad. Danger. This is bad. They corral oil with booms and conduct burnoffs, but everyone knows these mean nothing if the oil keeps coming. Finally, on May 4, British Petroleum proposes a way to stop the oil. The strategy stinks of the strange plans of desperation and reminds me of sketches on cocktail napkins: drop a four-story concrete structure over the leak. I imagine the word ACME painted on its side, an exaggerated sound effect as it plops into the ocean. Its name sounds like a sci-fi prison: containment dome.

The first mallard nests this spring failed. One behind a pile of ply-wood in the barn. One in the little A-frame duck house. One in the flower bed. Something got in, got the eggs—sad, pale-green shells broken open in the morning. Ducks persist. New nests showed up, all three in the barn. Duck nests are—I assume—built by ducks, but I've never seen one under construction. They do just *show up,* a bowl of straw or grass or leaves and feathers, then the eggs, one a day. The hen lays an egg in the morning, covers up the nest, and goes on with her business elsewhere until she has a nice clutch of ten or more. At that point, she settles in for good.

Ducks don't seem particular about location. The three ducks in the barn have chosen the following spots for nests: a gravelly dip along the foundation on the inside of the barn next to an over-turned clawfoot tub and practically beneath the rototiller; a space about as big as a shoebox squeezed between an old bit of cabine-try, two enamel sinks, a spare tire, a ladder, and the barn wall; and a patch of concrete floor that, when I pull my car into the barn at night, lies directly against my right front tire. The only things these places have in common are that they're somewhat dark and quiet, and they're in the barn.

The duck by the rototiller has a view of two mysterious parts of machines, perhaps a compressor and a radiator, as well as a broken sump pump, a broken shop vac, and a piece of metal sid-ing. She's made her nest of bits of straw and feathers and a few iris rhizomes that were in a paper bag nearby, but also, cleverly, from shredded pieces of old copies of the Cleveland *Plain Dealer* news-paper from 1933 that used to line a cooler in the storage area of the barn. I saved the newspaper because I wanted to read the ads. Her nest is architecturally eclectic.

The duck by the sinks has a view of virtually nothing, because it's rather tight and dim, and her nest seems entirely feathers, so many that it's hard to tell where the feathers end and the duck begins. She's the stillest of the three, blending in completely, mistress of disguise.

The duck sometimes under my car is well hidden in the evenings and morning when the car is parked but is sitting exposed in the middle of the concrete barn floor during the day. She's built her nest from leaves that had accumulated under the car, and I see her when I pull out to go somewhere, my headlights shining on a cranky bird. I relocated the nest a foot or so away from its original home when I became worried that I'd miscalculate my parking and run over the eggs. I carefully slid the nest along the barn floor, the hen snapping at me the whole time. She refused to follow the moved nest, returning to her original, now-empty spot. I picked her up and placed her on the eggs, where she decided to stay after all. If one of the clutches of eggs doesn't hatch, I'm betting it will be hers.

These nests illustrate one thing for certain: the barn holds a lot of junk.

When my dad and Cris finally decided to start cranking on the winch, tightening the cable attached to the upper corner of the barn, we weren't sure what was going to happen. There were really only three possibilities: the barn would straighten out, the barn would do nothing, the barn would fall down. From two of these possibilities there would be no turning back. As they cranked the winch, we could hear nails popping off boards inside the barn, percussive and resonant. After they'd given the winch a crank, they'd let the barn rest while we listened to the plinking of small things falling within. A few cranks into the procedure, my mom and I decided to go to the grocery store—some events should have few witnesses. We bought beer and potato chips and probably some other things that seemed like sustenance.

In high school physics, it took me weeks to understand vectors. I'd stare at those graphs, trying to conceive magnitude and direction. For about a month, as I struggled through problem set after problem set, I thought my life might be ruined by arrows. Then I snapped out of it and found salvation.

Seventeen days after the BP accident, the containment dome isn't working.

When I poke around the barn in the morning, I detect gentle peeping from over by the rototiller. Peeping means a hatch. I reach down so the hen will lunge to attack my invading hand, and beneath her she reveals a nest of several ducklings in various states of drying out. A day-old mallard consists of two parts— a head and the rest. They weigh nothing, their backs mostly black and their bellies yellow. From the instant they dry out after hatching, they run around and climb and behave like oversized, grounded bumblebees. They get into trouble. If you want to find all of the deep holes in your yard that you never knew existed, let loose a few dozen ducklings, and they'll proceed to fall into every one.

Fragility defines ducklings. I've learned to be prepared for small tragedies. A hen and her brood might go to the creek each morning, and each day she may return with one less duckling. A snapping turtle, perhaps, but everything kills ducklings. Even other hens. I've seen them grab ducklings that aren't theirs and break their necks. Cuteness and ugliness, a kind of yin and yang. And some ducklings just fail, can't get things right. They walk out onto the dewy grass of a cool spring morning and never warm up. I find them, try to get some heat back into them, but they die in my palm or on my lap as I work at my desk. I've made an effort to stop putting things on hold, losing hours, to try to save them, but a sick duckling is hard to ignore.

A month after the BP accident, just when the ducks are hatching, oil appears on shores, as tar balls or sheen, as fumes in the air, as a threat to the nests of the brown pelican. Nothing changes except the amount of damage. Now the government and the scientists and BP argue over how many thousands or tens of thousands of barrels of oil are contaminating the ocean each day. I have nothing to compare these numbers to. The only kind of barrel I know is a whiskey barrel, the kind one rides over a waterfall or wears when one loses one's pants.

When my mom and I got back from the grocery store, the barn was straight. My dad and Cris went to work making sure it stayed that way, with more cables and two-by-twelves and replacement studs and a lot of nails. Eventually, we would pour a new foundation. Eventually, we would begin to replace the cracked siding with new pine siding and configure spots for doors where the original doors once were. Eventually, we would be able to close those doors to keep things out of the barn, or at least most things.

The rototiller duck hatches ten ducklings, and, in a day, they leave the barn to wander the yard chasing bugs. I put out a small roasting pan full of water for them to swim in; ducks are insensitive to irony. I'm wrong about the car duck. A week or so after rototiller duck's eggs hatch, car duck's nest starts peeping. The next day, she waddles out with five ducklings. A small hatch, but something.

It's forty days after the accident, and BP announces that it may not be able to stop the oil for another two months, when it will have finished drilling two relief wells. A strategy with another ominous name—top kill—has failed. I've witnessed accidents that took place in a flash—a trailer of grain tipping over as it rounded a corner too tightly, a drunk man hit crossing a busy road, my own car careening into a snowy ditch—but they all appeared to unfold slowly, as though something could have been done to prevent them. Now we are all witnessing an accident happening slowly, and we're helpless.

June 4, and I'm standing naked in our kitchen holding a duckling. As he left for work, before I could get dressed, Cris handed me the little bird he'd found. Do I put down the duck to go find clothes? The duckling feels cold, barely moving, the runt of the rototiller duck's gang we'd been worrying about, though just yesterday it was running around eating flies. I turn on the oven so I can warm up a dish towel, scolding myself for not picking up a heating pad last time I was at the drugstore—something I only remember when I've got a duckling in my hand. The duckling doesn't lift its head. I go through the futile gesture of making warm sugar water, a trick that's never worked but also doesn't seem to do any harm. Wrapped in the dish towel, the duck stretches out its legs and rolls to its side, the duckling spasm I've come to recognize as inevitably preceding death. Placing the duckling on the stovetop, I grab another towel to heat so I can swap it when this one cools, but as I shut the oven, I hear a peep, a slight scratching. The end. I uncover the duck and set it on the kitchen table, then remove the second towel from the oven and go get dressed.

Last night, there were fifteen ducklings between rototiller duck and car duck. This morning there are nine. Cris discovered the dead bodies of four of car duck's babies by her nest in the barn, presumably killed by another hen, likely sink duck, who had tried to ambush rototiller duck's babies a few days ago. With the runt, this makes five dead and one unaccounted for. I head out to investigate. Perhaps in the night there was a battle over territory. The four ducklings lie belly up, light yellow fuzz exposed. Three have clear wounds—bloody heads, an eye popping out—the work of a strong squeeze to a delicate skull. Poking around for the fifth, I find its body underneath the workbench, a few feet from sink duck's nest. Then I notice something bright against the barn wall, the belly of another duckling, feet in the air. I'm not missing any more ducklings, so who's this? While I'm puzzling it out, the feet move, swimming upside down.

Junk. To get to the duckling, I have to crawl over a bunch of old storm windows stacked against the barn wall, a tight squeeze.

The sink duck is back there too, behind the sinks, sitting on her nest, hissing at me. The duckling looks fine when I pick it up, still breathing, kicking. But then I turn it over. The right side of its head appears crushed, a bloody hole in the fuzz toward the back, behind the eye, worse even than the injuries of the dead. Duck blood smells like fish or frog blood, the blood of a watery thing, slippery, algae-like. Also stuck to its wound is a substance that doesn't seem exactly to be blood. Brain? My first thought is to just get this over with, smack it with something, or give it a quick stomp. Then I think, what's the harm in bringing it in to a warm towel? The oven's still hot.

The latest oil strategy is called cut and cap. It involves slicing the pipe and putting a cap on it. BP made the cut on June 3, but it was jagged, which means the cap, if it can be placed, won't fit tightly. If these failures weren't so dire, they'd be almost slapstick, a predictable comedy.

We've tried many methods of keeping a duck warm. A heat lamp works fine usually, but sometimes it dries out a sick duck. A blow-dryer, not so good, for the same reason. A table lamp isn't warm enough. I often stick them down my shirt, between my breasts, and though it doesn't do the job any better than anything else, I want to believe it might feel more bird-like to the duck. At least, it makes me feel a little bird-like, the soft feathers over my heart. The warm towel is convenient if I have other things to do and can't sit around with a duckling in my clothes. There must be a way of figuring out the ideal approach—something about the latent heat of evaporation or the qualities of heat radiation. There must be a science to it, this restoration.

An hour and twenty minutes have passed since I discovered the injured duckling, and it's still alive, wrapped in a rotating sequence of heated dish towels, a sort of duck/towel enchilada. When I open up the towel, the duckling peeps, holding its bloody head up—a good sign. It's not drinking any water, though—a bad sign. I see two trajectories, arrows shooting off into the future, neither predicting what I'd planned for my day.

I've heard that if you want to knock down a barn, you should simply bust a hole in its roof. Time and weather will take care of the rest. The idea is that a structure will stand as long as its insides don't rot. Barns falling down fill the landscape of this country, bowing under their damaged roofs, like elephants collapsing in slow motion.

Our barn had a good roof when we moved in. Though some of the barn's supports were rotten at the foundation from termites, most of it was solid. The inside was dry. Once straightened, it could stand for years, decades, who knows how long.

Two and a half hours, and the injured duckling is still alive, although not much has changed about its condition. I'm not hopeful, but I'm not unhopeful. Based on my experiences with birds, I know a head injury isn't always fatal. Not much is fatal, really, except the inability to stay warm or a broken neck. Birds' brains recover. If a young bird will drink and eat, it will usually be okay. It sleeps and the brain mends. I heard about a study that found ducks can sleep while one half of their brain remains awake. Maybe my injured duckling doesn't need all of its brain to get by. It has scooted halfway out of its towel enchilada, and something is going on in that sad brain. Every time the duckling tries to lay its head down, it jerks it back up, unable to rest, alert. This could be a good sign or a bad sign.

Are these my ducks? Am I responsible for them? They're mallards, but they're mallards descended from five mallards we raised, mallards I bought at the feed store. Some hunters raise mallards and then release them so they can shoot them. Same with pheasants, quail. So they sell mallard ducklings at feed stores. I'd had a series of mallard ducks as a kid, most meeting ends of tragedy or mystery, and when Cris and I lived in Portland, Oregon, we had a pet Rouen for years. We drove her across the country when we moved to Ohio. Here, with a little land, I wanted more. The first mallards we raised had names—Lucky, Junior, Sop, Motorboat. Feed-store ducklings aren't sexed, and somehow all of these were hens. I could identify the distinct quacking of each, and each had her own personality. Finally, we ended up with a drake, Doodle, who got busy. For a year or so, they and their progeny stuck close to home. Then they flew off, spending less and less time in the yard, and eventually, somewhat on purpose, I lost track of which was which. I didn't want to know their fates. So they had nests. Their offspring had nests. They populate the rural ponds and creeks near our house. They linger between tame and wild, between something I've manipulated and something I can no longer control.

In the news, photographs of oiled brown pelicans, a dead dolphin, crabs crawling through sticky goo. Some experts suggest it would be better to kill the birds than to clean them, their survival rate is so low in the end. But other experts say that isn't true, and besides, we created this problem, we should do something. The containment cap BP installed captures some of the escaping oil. This is good, but the amount of escaped oil measured is much more than they thought had been leaking, which is bad.

We've seen all kinds of damage. If we'd brought some of the injured ducks we've nursed to a wildlife rehabilitator, they would've euthanized the birds. But maybe they *are* my ducks, and so I try. Who am I to make decisions about quality of life, about when to give up? I'm not trained in that field. We've had ducks attacked by hawks with holes in parts of their bodies. We notice them when they're walking around dazed from infection, and we catch them, searching for the wounds. Then we give them antibiotics and flush their injuries with Betadine, keep them in an old rabbit hutch we use for this purpose for a week or two. We've had a drake whose head was clearly in the mouth of something toothy for a few moments, feathers scraped off and a big scab over his skull, his neck floppy and weak. Same treatment—antibiotics, Betadine. We had a hen hit by a car one morning, and she emerged with a broken leg. I made a splint of soft bandages and kept her confined for a few weeks. All of these ducks healed, flew off, reentered the world of anonymity.

One duck, however, remains damaged. She flew in the night after Thanksgiving a few years ago. Her right leg was broken just below the joint and hanging on by only a little strip of skin and bit of tendon or other stringy flesh. The leg was starting to go bad above the wound. Her foot had no blood circulating in it. We knew we couldn't splint it and would have to take it off. We stood around the kitchen thinking this over. Our wine glasses sat half empty on the table. What to use? We thought of a knife but worried it might crush remaining bone. I opened drawers, surveying the instruments for anything sharp, our warm kitchen now a surgery theater equipped only with vegetable peelers, cheese spreaders, a lemon zester, a grapefruit spoon. Then I saw the poultry shears. I held her while Cris snipped off the lower leg. We brought out the Betadine and bandages. When she visits the yard every so often, she's unmistakable, lurching to the right as she wades across the grass. Standing on the whole leg, she dangles the half leg below her.

In the Gulf, teams of bird rescuers wearing biohazard suits scrub the birds. Some pour vegetable oil over the crude to make it lighter. The International Bird Rescue Research Center's preferred cleanser for the birds is Dawn brand dishwashing liquid, with its famous slogan, "Takes grease out of your way." Procter and Gamble gives it to them for free. They'll release the birds to unoiled shores in another state. They have no way of knowing how many make it.

Three hours, and the injured duckling is running around on the sunlit pine floor in a room off our bedroom. I don't know what to make of this. It's a little shaky, but its momentum seems to keep it going. I notice it's only moving clockwise, good side of head to the outside.

I decide to drive into town to the drugstore to get a heating pad. I can't spend all day rushing back and forth with warm dish towels. Outside, I notice car duck is in the yard with a duckling. Rototiller duck isn't missing any. Where are these extra ducklings coming from? Then it occurs to me—sink duck's eggs are hatching. My duckling is one of hers. In her frenzy, she attacked her own. When I get back, the duckling is scuttling around the room, but it quickly falls asleep on the heating pad.

My usual predictions are wrong. Forty-eight hours, and the injured duck isn't dead, but it still won't drink or eat. For two nights, I've gotten up every hour to reset the heating pad, which has an automatic shutoff timer. The duckling has a tendency to wander off the heating pad. On my knees in the dark, I reach around the floor until I find something fluffy. Each time, I expect to find it stiff, but each time it wiggles in my hand. Then one time I can't find it. Cris turns on the light, and there it is, on its back under the dresser, a faint scratching as it paddles its feet against the bottom of the dresser drawer. The wound on its head has stopped bleeding and formed a black crust. The duck's fuzzy face is a mask that ends abruptly at the scab.

The barn stands. Inside, it's easy to see how its structure has been reinforced, rebuilt—braces, cables, cement foundation. I try to envision it new and can't, as I take in its dark stench of duck shit and straw and eggshell. No more ducks in the barn. I'll keep them out, make sure they don't settle in. I'll impose order on this place, get rid of some of the broken junk.

June 6, and a plume of oil spreads underwater across the Gulf instead of floating to the surface. No one is sure why. It may be the one million gallons of chemical dispersants BP has applied to the spill. Experts argue over whether it should be called a plume or a cloud. The layers of potential damage grow. Experts talk of water columns, hydrocarbons, bacteria, molecular isotopes. No one can predict the effects of the accident. Even the experts can only guess at recovery—at the sea and shore's resilience—based on past recoveries. In the news, vacationers sunning themselves on the sand watch as workers collect tar balls.

About fifty-five hours after I found the duckling, it's finally beginning to show signs of wearing down. The energy it came with from the egg is running out. It can't walk but instead shuffles along the floor on its belly with its feet, swimming the wood, peeping in a way that seems cheerful to me. Outside, it's raining. I'm reading a book. The duckling stops peeping and twitches, rolling on its back, legs sticking straight out. Its eyes are open, blank and black. I reach down, and the body feels rigid. Then, inexplicably, the wings shudder, and the bird starts breathing. I curl my hand around it like an eggshell.

The afternoon passes on. Again and again, I find it on its back, legs out. Again and again, it breathes. I can't concentrate on my reading, thinking about the inevitable, about the little comfort I might give, about the impossibility of miracle. I think, if I knew more, maybe there would be something I could do. But I know this is hubris, to believe in control.

When BP drilled a hole in the ocean floor, it opened a hatch, a portal from a place of oil into a place of water. A hatched thing can't return to being unhatched, just like an idea can't be unthought. Drilled oil, a duckling, a plan—good or bad. A man opens the hatch and steps out onto moonscape, Earth in the distance, one moment in a complicated series of hatchings.

There's no way to know an undamaged world. How many pelicans would live without oil spills? How long will reminders persist? There's no way to calculate the span of damage for certain, only its magnitude and direction.

How many times can a thing reach the verge and return? How many times can I bear to watch? And must I? This duckling is the toughest duckling I've known. Yet I have other things to do—the usual messes to clean up. I leave the duck alone. Later, in the evening, fifty-seven hours after I found it alive, I find it again, a puff on the floor, finally dead.

the box

My father-in-law—as I think of him, though he died of complications from AIDS two weeks before our wedding—liked to keep things, and when we moved into his house in Portland, Oregon, to sift through the things of his life, we learned what he deemed worthy of keeping. Behind the back door stood a tower of egg cartons, floor to ceiling nearly, snuggly cupped together. On the back of the kitchen stove sat a can of questionable fatty drippings. The yard held an accumulation of things his neighbors and friends didn't want—railroad ties, broken cement, old bricks. In the basement on the workbench: a jar of instrument-grade mercury, a precipitate of his years as a chemist. He believed firmly in recycling, even if reuse meant simply saving something from being thrown out by storing it in his house or on his tiny lot. It was clear that he'd meant or hoped to use—to continue to use—some of the things we discovered, but for us, these things had no use and thus needed a new home, or at least a box in which to be kept. Some people keep things and some throw things away.

The foot-and-a-half-long pink rubber double-headed dildo we found in the bedroom was a problem. By now we had a shoebox full of similar things—cock rings and mysterious balls, smaller penetrating items. We'd labeled it with permanent marker, "Sex Toys."

But the dildo needed to be folded in half to fit into it and wouldn't sit still, insisted on popping open the lid like Jack in his uncomfortable box.

The box made its contents easier to handle, but we weren't sure where to go from there, weren't sure why we'd put these things in a box at all, except that in grief, there's already enough that's been lost. So the box ended up in the basement, the destiny of all boxes, inside another box.

I could say we forgot about that box, and we might have. We might have done something sensible with it, like thrown it away. But the labeling of the box implies that we had not thought of throwing it away. In fact, a month or two later, we contacted a man who bought estates to come by and look at some things we had described as miscellany. In our basement, I showed him a box that included, in addition to the labeled shoebox, a set of coffee mugs depicting frolicking elephants and polar bears engaged in suspicious behavior, a leather harness with rings, a small crystal penis, as well as some things of genuine value. I don't remember if he gave us any money, but he did haul it off. And so, having not thrown the box away, exactly, but instead shuffled it off into a new life, we felt questionably relieved.

As things left the house in similar boxes or, in the case of the truly purposeless, in one of the twenty truckloads to the dump, those most resembling my father-in-law, or at least how we chose to remember him, found their way into another box of sorts, a trunk, really. The act of putting something into a designated container makes its place in the world more permanent, and in this way we created our own kind of friendly ghost, the Dad trunk.

When we came across something useful only for remembering him—the cassock from his years as an Episcopal priest, for example, or the diary chronicling his struggle to make sense of his sexuality in the face of his calling—we put it in the trunk, piecing him together into a manageable size.

The size of a box matters, as everyone knows from wrapping presents. I feel almost ecstatic when slipping an object into the perfect box, just so, the flap of the lid holding it all tight. We kept a pile of boxes to put gifts in, boxes from irons and answering machines, boxes from gifts given to us—some having made the rounds of the family—all in promising sizes, locks for keys.

From among the pile's vast selection, only one box, the über-box, seemed like it would fit everything, but this particular box was never chosen. Whatever the gift I was trying to enclose—the wool sweater, the set of receiving blankets, the crystal wine glasses—when I reached into the pile, I pulled out *this* box, felt its heft and shape. *Yes! This box will do*—then the familiar disappointment as I read the label on its lid: "The Cremains of Joseph C. Teague." My father-in-law saved many things; though his lover's ashes were scattered a few years before on the Oregon coast, the box persisted, an empty grave.

Once, in my thirties, while standing in an antique shop with my dad, I noticed a scooter like the one I had ridden as a kid. The paint was the same steel blue, pearlescent, the kind of paint that makes a thing seem extra solid, like a bowling ball, but there were patches of rust from what looked like some form of repeated abuse. The tires were the same white rubber, though cracked and yellowed, and the white hand grips with the crisscross texture were chewed down. Over the rear fender, it too had a spring-loaded book holder, the scooter built in some faraway era when kids tooled around carrying stacks of books. Its likeness propelled me into the intense world of the driveway, the hours of scootering over chalk-drawn roads, the delicious dare of balance. I understood finally why older people frequent antique shops, calling out, "We had one just like this back on the farm," feeling in their hands the weight of heavy iron, of oily wood. I, too, wanted an accomplice of the past. "Dad," I said, pointing, "our scooter." He nodded, gave it a cursory glance, muttered something about how my younger brother had wrecked the frame jumping over ramps. He was deep into a box of woodworking planes and had no time for toys. Curious, I checked the price tag. "German scooter, circa 1950s. $75." When we got back to my parents' home, I told my mom about the scooter: "Just like the one we had. Whatever happened to that?"

My dad looked at me, confused, then bemused. "That *was* your scooter. Your mother sold it at a garage sale last year for five dollars."

Suddenly, growing old meant having my memories become a box of trinkets on a store's shelf, cryptically labeled in someone else's hand, outrageously priced beyond my budget.

My mom has chosen to fight battle with storage. Things in her house disappear silently, without regrets—memory requires no catalyst, no nostalgic trigger. When I was in my late twenties, she invited my sister and me to take what was ours from her attic or risk things being thrown out. Much of what was left was the remains of years of culling. I figured we were down to important papers from school, precious childhood toys, and favorite dresses. Some of the saved papers turned out to be not so important—for example, Sunday school worksheets with pasted-on depictions of Jesus Christ, followed, always, by a benevolent-looking sheep, or spelling lists of words no more than eight letters long, the effluvium of learning. A bit of shedding was indeed possible.

At one point that day my mom came across her own stuffed toy cat from girlhood, George, made with some brand of real fur, mangy with wear. She stuffed it into the black garbage bag, hardly pausing. I gasped. "But George!" I said, feebly unable to part with anything that was a proper noun. "He's better in my memory," she said. I know this was right, yet a fear of later needing even something like an unrecognizable stuffed cat keeps me filling boxes.

That same afternoon, I found a box marked "Mary's room" that seemed not to have been opened since its labeling. Inside were things I'd assumed, somewhat gratefully, had been tossed long ago, now eerily perfectly preserved, like a childhood friend from a long-ago neighborhood showing up in a dream, unchanged, wearing worn corduroys and baby fat, familiar but years out of place. Elf-bedecked kiddie stationary with letters half written in self-conscious cursive, stickers of garish rainbow shades featuring unicorns, a yellow pocket comb, the junk of trends long past—a random trove of embarrassing sentiments. Somehow the box had escaped several of my parents' moves uncensored, and as interesting as it was to see and smell and touch what should have been thrown away long ago and remember how I had wanted these things, how I'd used them, I wished they were already gone so I wouldn't have to decide their fates.

Because of the conflict between my inability to part with things and a strong dislike of accumulation, I was over thirty years old before I ever owned anything resembling a sofa. I tend to avoid buying a thing out of fear that someday I'll have to get rid of it. The attic is a kind of retirement home or hospice for broken or useless stuff. If I can just not get anything new, I think, I can care for these relics until someday they disappear of their own accord. The yearbooks I will never look at from the high school where I taught could potentially succumb to silverfish and their paper's acidity. The fabric I bought to make dresses that are no longer in style could be carried off by the perpetual generations of tube-shaped mice occupying the walls. The running shoes that aren't really good for running anymore, but aren't really worn out either, could be loaned to some houseguest for a muddy walk and get shuttled away in her luggage. It's also not unheard of for something to just get lost—inexplicably, fantastically gone.

I know this happens, and, while it irks me, a person who has been known to retrace her steps for blocks to find a lost button *and find it,* I think this vanishing may be the way I'll escape my problems with possession and dispossession. My husband and I speculate that during each of our moves, a box goes missing, and these missing boxes contain the things we've looked for and not found over the years—the drinking glasses, the wick for the small oil lamp, the cast iron skillet shaped like Texas, the colored print of *The Nymph of Spring,* the bike tire pump, the $200 in twenties withdrawn after the sale of our house in Oregon and meant to be travel money for the trip east to Ohio—things so exact in my memory, I might not really need them. This is the only explanation that makes sense to me. Boxes take things and sometimes don't give them back.

As for that perfect box, the one that would potentially hold everything, after a while, my husband got frustrated with always reaching into the pile of boxes and grabbing the last tangible resting place of the coherent remains of his father's lover. Got frustrated, likely, with me speculating how this or that person might react to getting a present in a box marked "cremains." He put the box to use, labeled it "picture stuff" and filled it with the various wires and hooks we use to hang framed things, little pieces of hardware that have a tendency, unboxed, to get lost on the workbench with the drill and circular saw and plane and other tools for which I'm fairly sure we have the boxes somewhere, just in case we want to put them inside, to see, if nothing else, if they still fit, to make them new again.

Isn't that what it means, "still in the original box," a thing preserved in a state of infancy? An object cuddled in its Styrofoam, waiting for love? The vitality of a thing seems proportional to its distance from its packaging. Maybe that's why mothers save their children's clothes. My own favorite dresses, preserved in my mother's attic, were doled out over time to my niece as she grew into them. I guess it's now my sister's job to keep these things or throw them away, and I'm glad. She's proven to be quite good at filling plastic-lidded tubs, at stacking them in her basement in a way that suggests a system, that indicates not packratishness but a plan.

For my part, I may have kept more boxes than I've kept things in boxes. There's the box that held the little birdcage that sits on the piano with the wind-up bird who used to sing before his mechanism wore out. There's the box from a wooden toy my niece and nephew played with when they were very small. There's the box an elderly friend sent to us filled with refrigerator magnets, a box she obviously had kept around for a while, as its original label was addressed from the Democratic National Committee to her husband, who had died several years before of Alzheimer's. There are, of course, innumerable shoeboxes, like the many that have served as coffins over the years for beloved pet birds. Sometimes I think of that carefully labeled shoebox, the one that slipped away, with its secrets, its evidence of illicit pleasures, of fecund life, and wonder if we should've held on to that one—maybe emptied it out, but kept the box.

the collection

For our sophomore biology collection projects, we had three choices—leaves, fungi, or bugs. The lazy kids chose leaves—no shortage of trees in Wisconsin. The only hard part was pressing the leaves flat. My older sister had done fungi her sophomore year, and for weeks, the house carried the dark-dust smell of spores as she dried her finds in the oven. Only a few of us picked bugs, those with time on our hands to scramble around with our net and lidded glass jar full of cotton balls drenched in ethyl acetate—the killing jar. Notice the -*ing*, kill*ing*. We needed a lot of bugs.

Of course, it wasn't a bug collection. It was an insect collection. Only one insect order—Hemiptera—contains what are called "true bugs," and why they are truer than the others, I don't know. Bed bugs are true bugs. The origin of the word "bug" is unclear. The word "bugger," though, seems to come from the Latin word "Bulgarus," meaning "Bulgarian" or, apparently, "heretic."

I was raised in the Lutheran Church, reciting the Nicene Creed: "We believe in one Lord, Jesus Christ, the only Son of God, eternally begotten of the Father, God from God, Light from Light, true God from true God, begotten, not made, of one Being with the Father." Begetting, the important distinction here. The Nicene

Creed was adopted in Nicaea in 325 AD and then revised in 381 AD at the First Council of Constantinople. The original essentially establishes that Jesus and God are on equal footing divinity-wise, and the revision expands on the whole Holy Spirit or Holy Ghost idea, which confuses me to this day.

Unlike the true God, true bugs don't get a capital letter. My favorite insect order isn't Hemiptera, though I do love cicadas, with their bulgy eyes and buzzing. As nymphs, cicadas suck on tree sap. Depending on the species, they can suck for two to seventeen years before they crawl out of the ground and up trees and discard their old skins. As kids, my sister and I would collect the root-beer-brown husks left stuck to tree bark after the shedding, crisp shells with the shape of the body intact, but split open from head to back where the adult emerged. We kept them piled in baskets on our dressers, the little hollow legs still clasping.

In order to get an A on the bug collection, we had to gather a certain number of insects representing a range of orders. I don't remember what the number was, but I do remember that I was determined to get an A, because I was an A student, and A students need to get As. Once we caught and killed the bugs, we were to mount them by piercing their bodies with pins and sticking them on a sheet of cardboard so that they would float above the surface, a host of shining exoskeletons.

According to my field guide, the insect orders of North America are as follows: Microcoryphia, Thysanura, Ephemeroptera, Odonata, Blattodea, Isoptera, Mantodea, Grylloblattodea, Dermaptera, Plecoptera, Orthoptera, Phasmida, Embioptera, Zoraptera, Psocoptera, Phthiraptera, Hemiptera, Thysanoptera, Megaloptera, Raphidioptera, Neuroptera, Coleoptera, Strepsiptera, Mecoptera, Siphonaptera, Diptera, Trichoptera, Lepidoptera, and Hymenoptera. Or: jumping bristletails, silverfish and firebrats, mayflies, dragonflies and damselflies, cockroaches, termites, mantids, rock crawlers, earwigs, stoneflies, grasshoppers and katydids and crickets, stick insects, webspinners, zorapterans, barklice and booklice, chewing and sucking lice, true bugs, thrips, dobsonflies and fishflies and alderflies, snakeflies, antlions and lacewings and mantidflies and owlflies, beetles, twisted-winged parasites, scorpionflies and hangingflies, fleas, flies, caddisflies, butterflies and moths, and sawflies and horntails and ants and bees and wasps. The names sound like tribes in a fantasy novel.

On a visit to the Cappadocia region of Turkey, near Göreme, my husband and I wandered around a complex of thousand-year-old churches carved from hills of volcanic rock—elaborate manmade caves. The hills were peaked, their conical tops carved by erosion. The churches inside had domes and columns and barrel-vaulted ceilings and apses. Some contained frescoes of biblical scenes. I had heard that the eyes of the figures in many of these frescoes were scratched out at some point by people worried about the Evil Eye. If that is true, I don't blame them. In the churches, people-sized trenches lined walls and floors—graves, empty. When someone died, they kept the body in one of these graves for a spell, then moved it to a permanent site. The graves came in different dimensions; the thresholds of doorways often held child-shaped graves. At one church, an iron gate blocked the door. Peering through, I saw a grave inside and recognized human bones. Then I realized I was standing next to a grave outside the door, a grave covered in a sheet of cracked Plexiglas—inside it, bits of bone and teeth.

The first bugs in my collection were common—American grasshopper, field cricket, blue bottle fly, silky ant, honey bee, two-spotted lady beetle. But then I had to start searching, picking up rocks, swatting at grass, lingering near lights in the evening. I had a couple of nets I'd borrowed from someone. One night, I saw my first golden-eyed lacewing, bright green, flapping its fragile wings along a dizzy path—slow, easy prey. How had I never seen one before? Twenty-five years later, I found a batch of lacewing eggs on an onion stalk, a line of dangling, individual threads, each capped by a tiny egg, a ladder of waiting life. How, too, had I not stumbled on these earlier? With each new bug in my collection, I asked myself the question: How had I missed this thing all these years?

The fall I collected bugs, I was fourteen, about to turn fifteen. By the end of the school year, my family would move away to another part of Wisconsin, but I didn't know this at the time. That fall, my world was familiar, and I was familiar to my world. I blended in well with the scenery.

On the same trip to Turkey, we toured Topkapi Palace in Istanbul, built by Sultan Mehmed II in the second half of the fifteenth century. It's full of displays of jewels, weapons, fancy clothes owned by the sultans, and relics (or purported relics) of religious significance, everything carefully cataloged. One of these relics is the rod of Moses. Another is the arm of John the Baptist. Both of these sound more exciting than they looked. The rod was essentially a stick. The arm, whatever was left of it, was encased in some kind of gilded metal, shaped like an arm and hand—pretty, but somehow dissatisfying.

I really wanted to catch a dragonfly—Odonata—for my collection. One afternoon, my mom and I headed with our nets over to a nearby county park to hike the trails and bag some bugs. I didn't usually hang out alone with my mom, without my younger brother or older sister. For some reason, this weekend she wasn't busy. The weather was sunny and mild, and we found a grassy slope where huge dragonflies buzzed just over us, swooping at our heads and then bolting in precisely the opposite direction. We lunged at them with our nets, but they'd spin away, only to return, tempting us. We jumped and jumped and jumped, waving the nets, and the higher we leapt, the more the earth felt like it was turning beneath us as we landed. At fourteen, I'd forgotten my mom could be so much fun. We didn't catch a single dragonfly.

Topkapi Palace also possessed beautiful mosaics and courtyards. In one courtyard, off to the edge of the property, broken pieces of ancient buildings littered the ground—decorative columns and basins and finials. They seemed to be waiting for someone to figure out where they belonged. When we were leaving the palace grounds, I noticed, near the gate, a giant abandoned-looking brick and stone building with dark arched windows and a central dome. It looked like it might've been a church, but I couldn't find a sign saying what it was or any entryway.

The Lutheran church I grew up in was ugly, like many Lutheran churches in the United States, which seem to embrace nonstandard church architecture. Maybe it has something to do with the Scandinavian influence. But churches aren't shelving units or dining room tables, and, in my opinion, should stick with arches and apses and stone and all that Gothic stuff. My church was round like a cake and covered in brown cedar shake siding. Triangular dormers poked out at regular intervals, with triangular windows of geometrically patterned stained glass. The roof was topped by an odd conical spike with a cross, reminiscent of a lightning rod. I was told as a kid that it was supposed to look like a crown. Jesus was King of Kings. But the only crown he wore was a crown of thorns, which was also ugly, so maybe the church was appropriately designed. Sometimes I have nightmares set in that church, and I'm running around and around its circular floor plan, from sanctuary to narthex to meeting hall to sanctuary.

The frescoes on the walls of the churches in Cappadocia depicted scenes from scripture, but not the scenes I think of when I think of Christian lore as portrayed on stained-glass windows, or at least stained-glass windows in more traditional churches. I think of plump baby Jesus on Mary's lap, angels draped in white cloth who look essentially like people dressed up as angels, lambs, groups of robed disciples lounging around chatting, a bloodless Jesus sad on the cross. Sometimes Jesus is kneeling and praying. Sometimes he's got his arms outspread and is gazing up at an invisible Heavenly Father, represented by sunbeams.

In the fall before the year I collected bugs, I was confirmed in the Lutheran Church. I'd taken two years of confirmation classes, once a week in the evenings. The first year, a classmate's mother taught us, and we spent almost the entire time reading a comic book version of the Bible called *The Picture Bible,* which was all a review for me because I already owned a copy and had read it several times. Almost everything I know today about the stories in the Bible comes from *The Picture Bible.* Illustrated by André LeBlanc, a comics artist who'd assisted Will Eisner on *The Spirit* and worked on classics like *Flash Gordon* and *Apartment 3-G,* the characters possessed Hollywood good looks. As a kid, I had a crush on King David, who could pass for Barry Gibb from the Bee Gees.

One church in Cappadocia, the Church of Saint Barbara, was decorated with designs painted in red ochre, including lines meant to give the impression that the church was built from stone blocks, rather than carved into the rock. On one wall, a crudely drawn rooster leaned over what was maybe a budding plant. Beneath it, a monstrous creature lunged, arms held up as though fighting or searching for a snack of brains. The thing appeared to have horns and a scaled belly. It also looked like it was painted by a five-year-old. A woman touring the church asked her guide, "Are these a child's drawings?" and I wondered why she would think they'd let a child draw on a church wall. The guide explained that this creature was a locust. Really, it seemed more like a cockroach.

The second year of confirmation class, we were taught by the church's pastor, Pastor John. He was in his forties, a handsome, bookish man. We had to memorize a lot of things from *Luther's Small Catechism*. We memorized the Ten Commandments and the explanation of each. "The Sixth Commandment: You shall not commit adultery. What does this mean? We should fear and love God so that we lead a sexually pure and decent life in what we say and do, and husband and wife love and honour each other." We memorized the Apostles' Creed and the Nicene Creed. We memorized the Lord's Prayer. We memorized definitions of the sacraments. We wanted to please Pastor John, who was a nice guy, so we memorized and memorized. But we were eighth graders on the verge of becoming high school freshmen, so we also goofed off.

When I said earlier that I wanted to earn an A on my bug collection, that wasn't exactly true. I wanted an A+.

The Picture Bible mentions locusts a few times. LeBlanc's illustration for one passage about a plague of locusts on Judah shows a man in scarf and tunic, waving his hands in the air at a small cloud of winged bugs. There's no illustration of the plague of locusts on Egypt in the Exodus story, though there are a couple of illustrations for the plague of frogs. Bright green frogs hop everywhere in the streets. It's not clear what damage they're doing. In one panel, a woman cries, "Ee-eek. A frog in my bread dough!" as a cute frog leaps into her bowl.

My bug collection grew and grew, my eyes always scouring surfaces for bugs. One night, I found an earwig on the wall of my bedroom. I found a silverfish among books in our basement, but it was too ephemeral to pin once dead. It seemed to be made of dust. I found a katydid and a praying mantis. Every bug went into the killing jar, then onto its pin. In order to get credit for each bug, I had to fill out a slip of paper containing order, genus, and species as well as collection location and date. I also collected Gary Larson's *The Far Side* cartoons about insects to include with my project. In one, two bugs stroll through a bug collection beneath dead insects on pins, and one says to the other, "God, I hate walking through this place at night."

The Church of Saint Barbara in Cappadocia is named after a saint whose father locked her in a tower as a young girl. I've read several variations of her story. The simplest version is that she was locked in the tower, converted to Christianity, and was then tortured and beheaded by her father, who was subsequently struck by lightning and killed. A more complicated version involves Barbara ordering some workmen to put three windows in a cistern her father was building, which somehow was a symbol of her faith, after which her father tried to kill her, except she was absorbed into the stone and transported to a mountain where she encountered two shepherds, one of whom betrayed her, and so he was turned into stone and his flock into locusts. But then her father caught her and put her on trial, after which her "paps" were cut off and she was led through the streets to be beaten. Finally, her father took her to a mountain, where she prayed and rejoiced, and her father beheaded her. Upon returning from the mountain, her father was zapped to the point where all that was left were ashes. The Catholic Church dropped the Feast of Saint Barbara from the liturgical calendar in the 1960s because it appeared quite possible that she belonged to the realm of legend and not history.

The churches in Cappadocia seemed to favor stories of violence, pain, and death. Shadrach, Meshach, and Abednego in the fiery furnace. Lazarus raised from the dead. The Slaughter of the Innocents. The betrayal of Judas. And of course, the Crucifixion. In one fresco, Jesus stands on what appears to be a demon, surrounded by spikes, chains, and a cross. Or perhaps these scenes stood out to me because they weren't the stories my own Christian upbringing lingered on. The gaunt figures, with their eyes scratched out, hovered over graves dug into the floor of the churches. A mineral urine smell emanated from the rock walls. No one would ever chirp "Jesus loves me, yes I know, for the Bible tells me so" in these churches. The only sound that I could imagine here was wailing.

It turns out the mysterious domed building on the grounds of Topkapi Palace is the Hagia Eirene, first built in the fourth century by Constantine I. In the late fourth century, the First Council of Constantinople was held there. The original church burned down and was replaced in the sixth century. What stands now was mostly constructed after earthquake damage in the eighth century, three hundred years before the Church of Saint Barbara was carved into the hills. Over time it's been a church, an armory, and a museum. Now it's a concert hall, though I didn't notice any signs for concerts. Hagia Eirene seemed like what, I suppose, it was—an empty building.

At another ancient church in Istanbul, the Chora Church, my husband and I tried to decipher the mosaics on the walls, which date from the fourteenth century. The angels float but appear to be only torsos, their robes ending where their waists would lie. A man covered in spots and wearing a loincloth appeals to a group of figures whose faces have fallen away with time. Another man stabs the throat of a bull, blood spurting. A seraph—a ball of wings surrounding a face—hovers over dead Mary. Christ descends into Hell and pulls Adam and Eve from their tombs, his hands clamping their wrists, the gates of hell beneath his feet along with Satan, bound, lying among his instruments of torture. Every visage seems sad—disappointed even. In one mosaic, guards rip a child from its mother's arms, stabbing it with a dagger, while another pins a child to the ground and slays it with a sword. A little higher up—I had to squint to see it—a guard hoists a naked child on a pike, which enters through its anus and exits through its head.

I needed one more bug for the A+, but how would I get it? I was running out of varieties. Then a neighbor who'd heard about my collecting brought over a perfect find—a walking stick. I'd only seen one once before. It was the coolest bug I'd ever held, its stick disguise perfect until it moved, crawling along my arm. It didn't seem to want to flee, unlike most of the other bugs I'd caught. Order Phasmida—ghost. I let it crawl around, watching how its legs balanced the stick body. I hesitated, but I wanted the A+. I put the walking stick in the killing jar.

I studied hard for the confirmation test. I knew I didn't want to fail—what would that even mean? I wanted to do my best. I memorized. When the time came, I demonstrated what I knew about all those commandments and creeds and prayers and sacraments on the exam, which included an interview about Lutheranism with Pastor John, and I passed. I had memorized well.

Despite my confirmation, I didn't take to religion. I drifted from the church, appalled at things I'd memorized nothing about, things I discovered were said and done in the name of Christianity. I didn't want to be included under that label.

Five years after my confirmation, Pastor John was removed from the church for having sexual relationships with women parishioners, including a close family friend, a lady I had a hard time imagining as a paramour. A year later, no longer religious, I was in Seattle, visiting a friend of mine from high school, whose family had moved from Wisconsin to Washington. I was twenty—relaxing in a hot tub, drinking a beer, and wearing a bikini. Apparently, Pastor John had befriended this family and followed them out to Seattle, because there he appeared before me, in street clothes instead of clericals, standing next to the hot tub. He didn't seem to sense my deep distress at his presence. What was I supposed to say to him? He knew what to say, though. He said, "I remember you got a perfect score on your confirmation test."

We believe we're one thing until we find out we're another, when the story we've been telling ourselves turns out simply not to be true. I didn't get the A+ on my bug project. One of my identification cards somehow went missing, so I was an insect short. I can't tell you how many times I've thought of my hubris and cruelty decades from that moment of realization. For nothing, I killed the walking stick, because I thought it would prove how much I'd learned. I didn't need the A+. I could've settled for the A, sub-perfect perfection. I didn't have to kill any bug, for that matter—I could've collected leaves. Instead, I put dozens of insects in the killing jar, pulled them out dead, and displayed them on pins. True bugs or not, they weren't saved, and neither was I.

project monarch

I remember them on everything—towels, coasters, school folders, T-shirts, posters, earrings, stickers, greeting cards, coffee mugs—orange and black and white wings symbolic of something, though I didn't know what. I was just a kid, and they were, I remember, everywhere.

Except they weren't. Now, decades later, when I go searching for the monarchs of the 1970s, I find few. Butterflies, sure. Lots of butterflies, many with psychedelic wing patterns not found on this planet. But not nearly as many monarchs as I recall. Searching through the stuff of my youth out there in the world, now antiques or collectibles or retro kitsch, I wonder where those monarchs went, or if I just made every butterfly a monarch in my mind.

My sleuthing turns up a monarch on an old latch hook wall hanging kit, that 1970s craft that had you using a metal hook to pull segments of yarn through a mesh backing to make a picture in a kind of shag rug. The latch hook monarch design shows an orange and black fuzzy blob with some fuzzy tan and fuzzy yellow blobs. In the photo on the package, it hangs in what seems to be a kitchen. A ceramic crock sits nearby, filled with a few wooden spoons, a whisk, a small strainer, but also with some dried stalks of weeds—a silly thing to store with one's utensils. The company that made it, Sunset Stitchery, also made embroidery kits, several of which feature monarchs, including one showing the very same scene as the latch hook hanging, much clearer when it's not in shag: the yellow blobs are dandelions. Monarchs do visit dandelions, but the weed they gravitate toward most is milkweed.

WEEDS

When I think of weeds, I think of a quote from Ralph Waldo Emerson. The words stick with me not because I feel they express some meaningful truth, but because they were printed on the foil package of an herbal tea I drank every morning one summer in the early 1990s. The quote as I've remembered it is, "A weed is a plant whose use has not yet been discovered." When I look it up to confirm my memory, it turns out that, like the monarchs, I've remembered it inaccurately. Emerson wrote, "What is a weed? A plant whose virtues have not yet been discovered." It's a question and an answer, not a statement, a "virtue" and not a "use."

Despite its poetry, the quote strikes me as naïve. A weed is a plant that is a pain in the ass in some way or another, usually due to its popping up where we don't want it—in cracks in the driveway, in flower and vegetable gardens, in lawns, in fields of crops. But almost all "weeds" have known virtues, and even uses. The leaves of pokeweed can be cooked and eaten when young (though they can also be highly toxic), and pokeweed berries have been used as dyes and ink for centuries. The plant has even been studied as a possible cancer therapeutic because it contains an antiviral protein. Lambsquarters make a nutritious spinach substitute, raw or cooked. Purslane is high in vitamin C and is used for tart salads. You can buy the seed from tony gourmet seed catalogs if it hasn't shown up on its own in your garden, as it has mine. Dandelions, of course, make good greens, and the petals can also be fermented for wine. And so on.

Of all the weeds I can think of, milkweed seems the most virtuous, if virtue and use mean basically the same thing. The stem's fibers can be used to make rope or fabric. The fluffy floss inside the pods can be used to stuff pillows or mattresses, much like down, but hypoallergenic. The milky sap contains latex. A fact I come across again and again, which seems truly virtuous, is that during World War II, milkweed silk was used as a replacement for the filling in life jackets, which was running low. Kids gathered the floss, and hundreds of tons kept soldiers from sinking into the sea.

At my home in Ohio, I've got a few acres of what I call "brushy field" on my property. Grass and crabapples and sumac and blackberry and goldenrod and Queen Anne's lace. Hundreds of trees we planted as tiny, foot-long whips—pine, spruce, tulip tree, oak, maple, cedar—are now twenty to thirty feet tall. But some spaces we've left treeless, and there, I cultivate common milkweed, *Asclepias syriaca*. Out of the tall grass, stalks sprout with broad, light-green leaves and nodding clusters of rubbery, orchid-pink flowers in summer, sweetly scented. The opening of the star-shaped blossoms, or umbels, makes me think of a firework exploding in extreme slow motion, starting with a tight ball of buds, which then flare out on tiny stems, drooping. When the milkweed is blooming, the yard feels soporifically heavy with fragrance. Monarch butterflies appear, gliding from one blossom to another. Then, after the flowers fade, a few prickled pods develop along the stems, growing several inches long, tapered at the end. When green, they are covered in fleshy spikes. As the months pass into fall, the plants dry and the pods turn velvety. Finally, they crack open, revealing tight layers of seeds attached to silk, which catch the wind and escape to drift across the field.

PRAIRIE

My memory, of course, is now established as suspect. But I remember the 1970s and early '80s as a celebration of dried plant matter, including bouquets of weeds in crocks. In Brownies, we wove hemp-like macramé hangers with beads like galls and wrestled corn husks into dolls. In the garden, Mom grew lunaria, which we called money plant, also known, for some reason, as honesty. Its flat seedpods transformed into clouds of circular, wax-paper-like "coins," perfect for arranging in a clay jar and collecting dust. I also recall, somewhere in our house, a bundle of dried wheat in a beer stein, wheat gathered from family land in Kansas, as well as a crock full of dried stuff next to our piano, which was in a high-traffic zone and always dropping bits as we shoved by. A bag of more dried stuff hung on the wall behind the bench where my sister and I sat at the kitchen table my dad had made by hand.

Maybe the dried plants grew out of the 1970s fondness for the prairie. The TV show *Little House on the Prairie* ran from 1974–82 and featured hunky Michael Landon as Pa Ingalls and Karen Grassle as his oft-sunbonneted wife, Caroline. Though her look on the show was fairly plain, Grassle exuded a kind of homestead hottitude, perhaps simply because of her proximity to smoldering Landon. The prairie was sexy. And so, apparently, were tiered and ruffled calico prairie skirts and high-necked, poufy-shouldered prairie dresses, trimmed sometimes with lace. Beyond fashion, the prairie popped up in kitchen appliances, in the popular hue Harvest Gold, Pantone color number 16-0948, that earthy brownish yellow. The name is probably supposed to evoke grains like wheat or oats, but it's pretty much the shade of dried weeds.

The prairie represented in *Little House on the Prairie* was mostly gone by the 1970s and had been gone for a long time. The government's Homestead Act of 1862 invited settlers to the prairie, giving away 160 acres per claimant for a promise to build a house and farm the land. Of course, that land was already someone's home: the Native populations who had lived there for thousands of years, who were then forced to move so the land could be "settled." Ma and Pa Ingalls converted the prairie to crops, as did my own ancestors, who were homesteaders in Kansas. Of all the prairie ecosystems that once thrived in the United States—240 million acres—sources say only 1 percent remain today, the rest replaced by agriculture. In some states, the loss is drastic: Iowa has only around .1 percent of its original prairie left, according to Iowa Prairies Network. A map illustrating prairie recorded in Minnesota from 1847–1908 compared to present-day prairie lands shows a big yellow swath of historical prairie bisecting the state from the northwest corner to the southeast edge. Existing prairies, marked in red, are speckles, amounting to only around 250,000 acres of the once 18,000,000 acres of prairie. I'll admit, I can't begin to picture what all that prairie must've looked like. I have a hard enough time grasping the area of my own 4.3 acres of land.

Of course, the *Little House* series wasn't filmed on the prairie but instead on Big Sky Ranch, a movie ranch in California, where, years later, some of the television series *True Blood* was filmed, featuring vampires instead of pioneers.

MIGRATION

Milkweed is named for its sticky, white sap, which oozes from the plant when the stems or leaves are broken off. The sap is poisonous to most, so creatures that nibble on milkweed ingest the toxins and are also poisonous. The monarch butterfly caterpillar eats exclusively types of milkweed. The butterfly lays eggs on the milkweed, and when they hatch, the caterpillars nibble for around two weeks, passing through five instar stages before they form a chrysalis. The instars—with their yellow, black, and white bands—remind me of little striped socks.

After spending ten to fourteen days as chrysalises, summer monarchs, if they survive, emerge, mate, and lay eggs. They live two to six weeks before they die. However, the last generation of butterflies to hatch east of the Rocky Mountains, in late summer, don't mate. Instead, though each butterfly is less than the size and weight of a Post-it note, they make the long migration to Mexico, where they winter over in huge colonies, clinging to trees en masse before mating. Come March, they'll begin flying north until they find milkweed upon which to lay eggs, which will become the first generation of the summer. Each new generation will then make its way farther, milkweed by milkweed, until the monarchs reach the northern United States and Canada.

MEMORY

Those monarchs I remember from the past must be hiding somewhere. I dig around the yard sale of the internet some more and discover a few. Stylized on a pale-yellow coffee percolator. On a cotton dish towel with other blue and yellow butterflies and some flowers I recognize as lupine, as well as some flowers I don't recognize as any real variety. Across pale-blue wrapping paper, encircled in the words *Birthdays are sunlit times of joy and new beginnings.* But where I find them the most is in clusters on glassware, orange wings bright, for sale on eBay and Etsy, where they wait for new use. In the end, though, I find many more 1970s owls and mushrooms than monarchs.

I also find floating around on the internet a few articles about something called Project Monarch, but these stories are decidedly not about monarch butterflies and instead are about an alleged government mind-control experiment run through the CIA's Project MKUltra program. I skim some articles, eyes landing on phrases such as "trauma response" and "multiple personality disorder" and "slave" and "master" and "marionette programming" and "Illuminati" and "demon possession." I linger over the number of Americans purportedly subjected to Monarch programming—two million. According to one source, the subjects can be called up by handlers to perform tasks—like assassination—that they later won't remember, and will commit perfunctory suicide if discovered. One article suggests that the name "Monarch" comes from the fact that monarch butterflies carry out a year's migration cycle, through the multiple generations, *as though programmed.*

SOULS

One image of monarchs from the 1970s that passed under my eyes as a kid was the August 1976 copy of *National Geographic.* On the cover, a woman dressed in a blue denim shirt and jeans sits among thousands and thousands of monarch butterflies. Butterflies rest on her dark hair, pulled back in a bun. Butterflies cover her feet and lower legs. A few orange blurs of butterflies fuzz the foreground. The surface where she perches flutters with fragile wings. Were she to move, it seems she would crush hundreds, but she's motionless, her arms stretched out before her, where butterflies land.

The woman is identified as Cathy Brugger. She was young and Mexican and married to an older American, Ken Brugger, with whom she conducted research. "Cathy" is what Brugger called her, but her given name was Catalina, and her name now is Catalina Trail.

Until 1975, North American scientists had no idea what monarch butterflies did once they entered Mexico. All scientists knew was that the monarchs crossed the southern Texas border and then, *poof,* disappeared. Where they went next was a mystery.

I'm fascinated by the existence of this hole in our understanding of something as ubiquitous as a monarch. Sure, there were some scientists trying to figure it out, including Canadian Dr. Fred Urquhart, who hired Catalina and her husband Ken as research assistants. But what about the rest of us? Was anyone curious? Or were we just content to have the monarchs show up each summer, reassuringly reliable, like water from the tap?

In January 1975, Trail and Brugger found the monarch wintering grounds, in the Sierra Madre Mountains. Millions of butterflies clinging to the evergreens. The article by Urquhart accompanying the cover photo barely mentions Trail, except to say, "Ken Brugger doubled his field capacity by marrying a bright and delightful

Mexican, Cathy." Here, too, is a hole, something missing; she was more than just a pretty model for the cover.

I consider why the *National Geographic* article leaves out Trail's role in locating the butterfly wintering grounds. According to an interview with Trail, she worked side by side with Brugger from the start, beginning in 1973, before they were married. But the article is written by Urquhart, the Canadian scientist, who perhaps didn't understand how involved she was in the search, her contributions. Perhaps. Or perhaps he simply didn't want to spread the credit around too much. Or, perhaps, because she was young and a woman and Mexican, she didn't fit his idea of who belonged in the story, a story he might have felt he owned, since through his tagging, he had tracked the butterflies to Texas and projected the location of the wintering grounds in Mexico.

I want to admire him as a scientist, but I'm put off by her absence in the article and by one passage, describing when he first saw the butterflies in Mexico, in 1976, a year later: "I had waited decades for this moment. We had come at last to the long-sought overwintering place of the eastern population of the monarch butterfly. Every wide-eyed child and meadow walker in the eastern United States and nearby Canada knows this colorful butterfly, by sight if not by name. . . . But in winter the monarch vanishes from the regions. Where does it go? Until now, no one had known." He makes it sound like he was the first to realize the significance of the wintering grounds, not Trail or Brugger, nor the people native to the area, who had always noticed the clouds of monarchs each year as they arrived—an event that coincided with the Day of the Dead—and who believed the butterflies represented people's souls.

MISSING

In 2013 I was standing in my yard mid-July, staring out across the milkweed, when it occurred to me that I had yet to see a monarch. Usually they begin to show up early summer. Their absence drifted across my brushy field, alighting on my consciousness. Where were they? Eerie, to have something usually so common now an omission in the landscape. I knew about threats to their wintering grounds such as logging and conversion of forest to agricultural land. A drought in the South wasn't helping, either. But this seemed drastic, not a slow trickling away.

As it turns out, the migrating monarch population has declined by 85 percent since the mid-1990s. In the Midwest, surrounded by animals, plants, and people who pull through tough winters and scorching summers, it's easy to think of extinction as something that happens far away. We're not fragile here. But of course, the passenger pigeon, once so plentiful the flocks would block out the sun, lost its battle with extinction in the Midwest, the species dying out with the last bird in an Ohio zoo in 1914.

It's easy to think of extinction as someone else's fault, some tragedy brought on by things beyond our control, like the economic struggles of a poor nation far away. It's easy because then we're off the hook and can watch, sad but guiltless, as, say, the Southeast Asian Sunda rhinoceros population dwindles to a few dozen, mostly killed for their horns, including the last of the Vietnamese population of the species, shot in Cát Tiên National Park in 2010 by poachers.

But look closer. The Sunda rhino owes much of its fate to our deforestation of Việt Nam using napalm and Agent Orange during the war, which obliterated the population to such an extent that in the 1970s, it was thought to be extinct.

Now, look closer at the missing monarchs, and you'll find our love of cheap fuel. You'll find hamburgers, chicken wings, hot dogs. You'll find soda and candy and cookies. You'll find T-shirts. Ethanol, animal feed, high-fructose corn syrup, oil, sucrose. Corn, soybeans, cotton, sugar beets. The United States grows around 91 million acres of corn alone. Another 86 million acres are planted to soybeans, and 10.9 million to cotton. The percentage of corn that is herbicide tolerant is almost 90 percent, and the percentage of soybeans is 94 percent. Cotton is 95 percent. Herbicides kill weeds, and herbicide-tolerant crops can be sprayed with non-selective glyphosate, and survive, allowing for widespread use on fields.

When I think of these numbers, I try to envision at least 163 million acres of land in our country that are essentially weed-free. I can't quite fathom it. Of course, there are other herbicide-tolerant crops besides corn, soybeans, and cotton, so the number is even higher. But 163 million acres is a significant chunk of the 240 million that were once prairie and had weeds aplenty, including the monarch caterpillar's only food, milkweed.

I look at the label of Enlist Duo, a glyphosate herbicide from Dow made for herbicide-tolerant Enlist corn. After involved descriptions of general precautions ("Keep out of the reach of children," "Avoid contact with skin"), operator use precautions ("Keep and wash personal protective equipment separate from household laundry," "After work, remove all clothing and shower using soap and water"), physical or chemical hazards ("This gas mixture could flash or explode"), first aid ("Rinse skin for 15–20 minutes"), toxicological information ("No specific antidote"), environmental hazards ("Toxic to small mammals, birds, aquatic organisms and non-target terrestrial plants"), leaching ("The use of this chemical may result in contamination of groundwater particularly to areas where soils are permeable"), and disposal ("Do not reuse this container for any purpose")—after all of these warnings and risks come long lists of over one hundred weeds Enlist Duo will eradicate, including lambsquarters, purslane, dandelion, and common milkweed.

None of this is a surprise to me—the toxic nature of herbicides, the vast species they can kill. Aren't most of us aware of the dangers of chemicals? More aware even, perhaps, than we are of the virtue of weeds?

VIRTUE

What is virtue? The Platonic virtues are temperance, prudence or wisdom, courage, and justice. In addition to these four "cardinal" virtues, the Catholic catechism espouses the "theological" virtues of faith, love, and hope. The seven heavenly virtues, in opposition to the seven deadly sins, include diligence, patience, chastity, kindness, temperance, charity, and humility.

The general definition of virtue includes these principles, but everyone has their own variations on the theme of what is good. Benjamin Franklin was a fan of silence, cleanliness, and order. The Romans, apparently, valued manliness and sternness, as well as humor. Hinduism appreciates freedom from anger and control of one's senses, among other things. Buddhist virtues include equanimity, or balance in the face of life's many contrasts, such as loss and gain. When I consider these characteristics, I think about the many I don't possess. I also think that, except for silence and diligence, weeds have a hard time demonstrating any of these virtues.

Maybe, Ralph Waldo Emerson, "use" is in fact a better word. We're the ones who may or may not be virtuous, and how we use something reflects our virtue or lack thereof. The seven deadly sins are lechery, gluttony, greed, sloth, wrath, envy, and pride— several of which seem to drive how we use our land, or maybe how chemical companies say we should use our land. Even while they tout the effectiveness of herbicide-tolerant crops, they admit that weeds are becoming resistant to glyphosate. Without new options, farmers use older, more harmful herbicides. Even if there were new options, one article by a DuPont agronomy research manager states, "Overreliance of any new weed management tool will eventually lead to its failure." We're prideful to believe we can control nature without consequence.

RESERVE

Catalina Trail and Ken Brugger encountered their first monarch wintering ground high on the steep peak of Cerro Pelón, located along the border of the states of Mexico and Michoacán. The area where the butterflies winter is now the Monarch Butterfly Biosphere Reserve, created by the Mexican government in 1986 in order to protect their habitat and now encompassing around 139,000 acres and eight winter colonies.

By "created," I mean that the government imposed restrictions for land use on the people to whom the land belonged, the ejidos—collectives formed by the government in the years after the Mexican Revolution, consisting of the people who had been peons working the land on haciendas, earning little and accumulating debt to the rich hacienda owners. The haciendas were clearly exploitive, demonstrative of several deadly sins. On the other hand, while the ejidos certainly have their virtues, I find them confusing, a messy system resulting from efforts to right some horrible wrongs, to enact some justice. For instance, not all members of the ejido have the right to own land or vote. Those that do, the ejidatarios with voting rights, as I understand it, generally pass their rights on to a single descendent, often at death, leaving the younger members of a community without much say in the decisions of the ejido. I imagine that the ejidatarios living in the Biosphere Reserve with rights must remember life before the reserve, while the younger community members without rights do not. If anyone is bitter about the impositions of the reserve, it's most likely those who can make decisions.

Limitations have been placed on the activities the ejidos in the butterfly reserve can undertake, such as logging, which helped sustain generations before the creation of the reserve. Some people still engage in illegal logging, cutting trees in what is known as the nuclear zone, where the butterflies winter, and elsewhere, even when they aren't supposed to. The ejidos are quite poor, and while I'm frustrated at the loss of monarch habitat, I can't call such logging greed.

ENCOUNTER

It's March 20, 2015, and I'm bumping along on a brown and white speckled horse, up and up and up a rocky trail, climbing the side of Cerro Pelón. I'm with my husband and our guide, Vicente, a man in his thirties. We're here very late in the season. The butterflies had left by March 21 last year, so I'm not sure I'll get to see what I've come for. Vicente is from the town of Macheros, which lies at the edge of the butterfly reserve. The horses belong to a man in town. Everyone in the community who wants to rent out their horses to visitors of the reserve is on a list, and when their name is up, their horses go.

In Macheros, we're staying with Vicente's brother, Joel, who, along with his American partner, Ellen, runs a small inn. There are ten children in Vicente and Joel's family, and three of the five brothers have spent time as undocumented workers in the United States, doing landscaping, factory work, and other jobs. I imagine their own dangerous migrations north, their returning home. Joel worked in a nail salon in New York, earning good money and generous tips, with which he built his house in Mexico. He returned to Mexico after eight years but then considered going back to the United States. When I ask him why he would take the risk of crossing again, he says that after all that time away, he didn't feel like he belonged in Macheros. But then he met Ellen, who had come to see the butterflies, and they started their business of butterfly-related tourism. They hope that if the village can see that butterflies bring as much income as logging, they'll be more invested in protecting the reserve. The pitch has not always been easy to sell. Investment in tomorrow is tough when you're hungry today.

The trail zigs and zags along the mountainside, where tall evergreens stretch high around us. The horses snort and balk. The path is cluttered with fist-sized rocks and tree roots, and the horses' hoofs slip occasionally, despite their careful footing.

Vicente speaks better English than I do Spanish, having

worked in the United States, and we all chat back and forth in a mix of both. He's a fun guy. He tells us a story about how when he was a boy his father took a family of tourists up the mountain, and on the way back down, one of the tourists, an older man, had a heart attack and died. The dead man was riding Vicente's mare, and the news made him cry, because he worried something might be strange about his horse now that a person had died on her. "My horse!" he says, laughing. The dead man had been hospitalized before the trip but chose to come up the mountain anyway. "At least he saw the butterflies," Vicente says, and I'm not sure whether or not he's being ironic.

About an hour and a half up the trail, he gets excited, "Do you see? Do you see?" I don't. Then I do. An orange flutter on the edge of my eyesight. Then another, resting on the branch of a bush. Then more, flickering in the air along the trail. These bright wings encourage me.

A GESTURE

It's mid-July and eighty-nine degrees. A few weeks earlier, the first monarch I'd spotted this summer floated around the yard, visiting my milkweed, including a few stray plants coming up in a flower bed by the back porch. I've seen only one or two since then. I'm pulling weeds, virtuous or not, when I glance at one of the milkweed leaves. On it, about an inch long, a tiny striped caterpillar is chewing the most tender top shoot. I scan my brushy field, where the hundreds of milkweed plants are blooming. At the edge, I see a second, the same size. I look and look, but that's all I find. Maybe these are the first. The next morning my searching turns up a third and a fourth, chewing their way through leaves in my garden and field. A single monarch flits over the field, lands on the floppy blossoms. Part of me wants to coddle the caterpillars, pluck them with their leaves from the plants and keep them safe, but the rest of me knows this would be only a gesture, and a small one at that. But I try to track the ones I see.

Two of the smaller ones disappear, long before they are large enough to transform into chrysalises. A third, larger caterpillar vanishes, and may or may not have gone off to find a place to meta-morphose. I want to think it has. So I reach for that small gesture and put the last caterpillar inside in a large vase with fresh milk-weed, set it on my porch, and watch it eat for a few days. A few nights later, it climbs to the screen I've stretched over the top, spins a little silk, drops down into a J-shape, and hangs there. I stay up late hoping to see it transform. In the morning, it's still a caterpil-lar, but when I'm not looking, it becomes a bright green chrysalis with a row of tiny gold dots—a jade pendant. Inside, the caterpillar has turned mostly to stew. Were I to cut it open, I'd find black ooze. In ten to fourteen days, the chrysalis should start to darken, and the shapes of wings appear. At that point, it will be ready to open.

Just as we're about to leave town, the chrysalis begins to darken. I take it outside and attach it to a small branch. When we return from our trip, a clear chrysalis hangs, broken open, butterfly-less.

WONDER

On Cerro Pelón, we dismount the horses and stare, standing in a cleared area where the trail widens, flanked by oyamel trees. In the trees are clusters and clusters of monarchs. The air is cool, and the monarchs are fairly still. They cling to the branches, their closed wings dangling, pale on the outside, so they appear covered in frost. When their wings open—a flash of the familiar orange. A ranger approaches us on foot. It turns out he's Vicente's cousin, and he leads us over to a roped-off trail, a little farther down the mountain. I hesitate, thinking about the purpose of the rope, rationalizing that he is a ranger and wouldn't do anything to harm the butterflies. But fleetingly, I worry he might just want to make a few tourists happy.

I duck under the rope, take just a few steps, and I'm surrounded by butterflies—in the trees, on the ground, flicking in the air. In places, it is, in fact, very much like the picture in *National Geographic,* at least within the frame of my perspective. The bounty is an illusion. The butterflies' total Mexican wintering grounds have gone from 44.5 acres in 1996–97 to 2.79 acres in 2014–15. In 2013–14 the monarchs gathered on only 1.65 acres, an area the size of a large suburban lot. So there's been a slight rebound, of over an acre, but I can actually picture an acre, and it's not very big. On land that totals fewer acres than my property, all of the migratory monarchs wait through the winter.

I'm not thinking about acres, though, in the moment. I'm thinking about the sound, which is the soft flutter of uncountable wings flapping. As the sun warms the trees, clouds of butterflies erupt into the sky, brushing my face and hair and arms. I'm horrified that I might crush them as I move. They're both fragile and incredibly tough. Some of their wings are tattered. Some lie dead on the ground—many, Vicente tells me, males who have already mated, but also bodiless wings, victims of mice. We linger in the oyamel for about two hours, alone with Vicente, his cousin, the sheaths of wings in the trees or transparent and illuminated in the air. Then another group of tourists approaches, and we head back down the mountain.

On the trail, we pass stumps of logged trees I'd noticed earlier. I ask Vicente about them, and he tells me that they were probably already dead when they were cut down. I wonder.

SEEDS

September. Monarchs begin migrating over Ohio, pausing in places along the edge of Lake Erie before continuing on. For a few days, I see them pass through, flickers of orange along the road, heading south. Then, out in my brushy field, another caterpillar. I bring it in, put it in the vase, watch. It hangs in a J after just a day, and the next evening begins to transform from striped worm to green case. Even as I watch it slip from one state to the other, it seems impossible. And then I wait. And wait. Two weeks pass. The green chrysalis does nothing. I worry something has gone wrong. But since I don't understand what happens even when things go right, I'm not sure what might cause things to go wrong. A few more days pass, and then the chrysalis darkens. The next night, we watch as the butterfly emerges, a fat abdomen and wrinkled wings. She pumps her body, sending fluid into her wings, which unfold and hang, drying. Then she slowly opens them. Male butterflies have black spots on their hind wings, so I can easily tell she's a female. In the brisk morning, with the temperature in the low fifties, I place her on the purple blossom of my butterfly bush before I head to work. She's a late fall butterfly, bound all the way to Mexico, where she'll winter, perhaps at Cerro Pelón. She's gone when I return, and the next day brings high winds from the north. I wish her luck.

After I release my butterfly, the US Department of Agriculture releases some news. In November 2015, the government announces it will spend $4 million dollars to increase butterfly habitat in ten states along the corridor the butterflies travel: Texas, Oklahoma, Kansas, Missouri, Illinois, Iowa, Minnesota, Wisconsin, Indiana, and Ohio. The basic idea is to encourage farmers (called "producers" in the release) to plant butterfly-friendly plants. Participation in the program is voluntary, and producers receive some financial assistance. A producer can learn more by reading a dense, chart-filled USDA brochure titled "Biology Technology Note No. 78, 2nd Edition: Using 2014 Farm Bill Programs for Pollinator Conservation," which features on its cover photos of two monarchs feeding on a plant that is not milkweed. You can also read a more general brochure from the USDA titled "Monarch Development Habitat Project," which also has a monarch on its cover, feeding on a weed that is also not milkweed. The goal of these programs is to increase the North American monarch population to 225 million by 2020, with an overwintering population covering fifteen acres in Mexico.

If you read the more general brochure, you'll find out that common and swamp milkweed are the most important milkweed plants for building monarch habitat. But you also find out that no variety of milkweed can be planted with crops or in pasture, because its milk mucks up machinery and also makes livestock sick. So if producers are going to plant milkweed, it will have to be on land that is part of what are called "cropland retirement programs," or land not in use for production. The benefit to the producer will have to outweigh no longer having the land in production. The land will have to be more useful to the producer as weeds. Considering this, I wonder if "sacrifice" is a virtue and if it is one "producers," whose name suggests they are defined by their products, embrace.

ECLOSURE

The monarch is a popular cause, the butterfly a perfect spokes-insect for conservation and caretaking, sweet and unthreatening. Species like the monarch are known as charismatic species, valuable for environmental education because they appeal to the general population in ways other more effective pollinators, such as stinging bees, do not, even though bees are more useful. Monarchs also suggest a solution an individual can partake in, so it doesn't surprise me that many of the articles I find about monarch butterflies tell of folks raising caterpillars in their homes or of schools planting milkweed. I don't find much about producers volunteering to bring back millions of acres of missing weeds.

When I last sat among the oyamel on Cerro Pelón watching the butterflies in early March 2020, I had no idea what the next year would bring. Now, the USDA's 2020 goal has come and gone, unmet. Overall, the 2020–21 season was a hard year for the butterflies. The coronavirus pandemic resulted in the closure of butterfly reserves and a sharp decrease in the number of tourists migrating to the communities that make a living hosting them, dropping from almost half a million the year before to eighty thousand. With few visitors, the biosphere suffered from increased illegal logging, losing thirty-three acres of trees. Without the oyamel trees, no amount of milkweed will save the monarch. But planting a little milkweed in one's flowerbed is an easier, if less effective, way to feel virtuous than fixing a lopsided system of wealth and greed. Still, I try to see each small patch of milkweed I notice tucked along lawns and gardens as a symbol of shared diligence— or maybe humility.

The US Fish and Wildlife Service could make all of this less virtue-reliant by listing the monarch under the Endangered Species Act, a proposal currently under review following a petition to categorize the butterfly as "threatened" in 2014. In 2020 they determined that the butterfly's listing was "warranted but precluded," which means that other species are a higher priority, and the butterfly's status will be reviewed annually. But part of me wishes virtue could simply win out, that the prairie might be restored because of its own allure. Maybe we will return to the sexy days of 1970s weed worship, the lusty stalks whipping along the calico hems of ruffled dresses, hinting at strong thighs.

It's winter, and I'm driving through my little Ohio town, passing by an intersection that holds an out-of-business carpet store, a gas station, a Baptist church, a candy shop. Waiting for the light to change, I notice a black SUV pull to the corner of the candy shop parking lot, where a patch of weeds grows next to a split rail fence along the road. A woman climbs out. I assume she's going to stick a sign advertising a yard sale into the ground, since yard sale signs flutter on almost every corner around here. Instead, she steps toward the patch of weeds—milkweed, I see now, the pods dry and gray. She snaps off a handful of stems and stuffs them into her back seat, then hops in and slips away. The rest of the story I can only imagine.

songs of the humpback whale

When I was a kid in Wisconsin in the 1970s, we didn't have global warming. We had litter, and we had pollution. Well, and nuclear annihilation, but we didn't really learn about that until fourth or fifth grade, and even then it didn't make a lot of sense. We did have endangered species. And of course, man-made extinction, but those dodos and pigeons were long gone, so it was kind of hard to grasp what we'd lost.

About these problems, there were things we could do and not do. Do: make a yearly trek down the road with a garbage bag to pick up beer bottles; avoid killing things; plant trees. Don't: throw candy wrappers out the window; leave toilet paper in the woods; deep-six soda cans in the lake. Don't: leave the lights on when you aren't in a room; burn stuff that's plastic; own a factory. Do: listen again and again to the 33 1/3 RPM, six-inch flexi disc *Songs of the Humpback Whale.*

On February 24, 2017, I shared a picture of my blooming *Iris reticulata* bulbs on Facebook. They started blooming on February 21, the earliest by a week they've ever bloomed in my northeast Ohio yard. A lot had sucked about the previous few months, and it cheered me to have a week of warm weather that coaxed the flowers to pop—deep purple, pale blue, sunshine yellow—their velvety petals dropping open, speckled like Gerard Manley Hop-kins's "dappled things." Within minutes, a friend commented that his snowdrops were flowering and that his walnut was budding out. "What does that portend?" he asked. I replied, "It sounds like it means that someday there will be shade." He responded, "Or that they will freeze and fall off." On each flower post some-one shared, for every "Pretty!" comment, there was at least one "Oh no! Too early!" Then it got good and cold again, and everyone calmed down.

Songs of the Humpback Whale was included in the January 1979 issue of *National Geographic,* accompanying an article titled "Humpbacks: Their Mysterious Songs." The album was pressed on a floppy black square of vinyl, and our kiddie record player had a hard time keeping the speed even—speeding up and slowing down as the needle circled the grooves. The National Geographic Society pressed 10.5 million copies of the flexi disc, or sound sheet, the largest single pressing of a recording to this day. On the recording, zoologist Roger Payne narrates over echoey moans and chirps and squeals of whale songs, which he explains are "prob-ably the longest, loudest, and slowest songs in nature." When I heard these songs in 1979 at the age of eight, I had no memory of seeing the ocean, which I'd visited when I was very small. The noises suggested a huge space, an infinite and dark concert hall. When people try to explain size to kids, they often rely on a famil-iar unit of measure, the school bus. A female humpback whale is about the length of 1.25 seventy-two-passenger school buses. The much bigger endangered blue whale is the length of over 2 school buses and weighs more than 15 school buses. The average depth of the ocean is around 310 school buses, or, if you would like to be confused, 242 humpback whales.

We didn't hear about global warming back in the 1970s, but we did have "inadvertent climate modification," which sounds like someone accidentally bumping the thermostat—and pretty much is. Scientists figured we could affect climate but weren't sure in which direction. Aerosols cooling versus greenhouse gases warming? Then, in 1979, the same year as the release of *Songs of the Humpback Whale,* the Charney Report, a study by the National Academy of Science, used the term "climate change" in its discussion of the impact of increasing carbon dioxide on the planet. The report found "no reason to believe these changes would be negligible," a mild and unlyrical way of saying bad things were probably afoot. Global warming usually refers to surface temperature issues, while climate change covers that warming as well as other impacts of greenhouse gases. Nowadays, the term "global climate change" means everything we should wisely fear.

Litter, when I was a kid, was beer bottles and soda cans, Styrofoam cups, candy wrappers, paper products. When we'd scour the ditches on our quest for garbage, we were mostly fishing out cans and bottles. On both sides of the road near my house lay wetlands, the marshy western edge of Lake Keesus's Marquardt's Bay, and we'd pluck things out from among the cattails. I don't remember finding fast-food detritus, but that may be because there was no fast-food restaurant within miles and miles of the place. Six miles away, in Hartland, there was an A&W drive-in watched over by a big fiberglass bear who wore a sweater and no pants, and in the parking lot, for some reason, a chain-link pen holding a real llama. You got your root beer float in a big glass mug. I couldn't tell you how far away the nearest McDonald's was—too far for a kid on a bike.

I also remember pulling out plastic six-pack rings, which made me feel particularly helpful, since we were told they could strangle ducks and turtles. We knew that we were supposed to cut up the rings when we threw them in the trash, I guess to protect the wildlife in the landfill. I didn't really think it through. After outcry about the rings harming wildlife, manufacturers switched to rings that were "degradable," which meant that they became brittle in sunlight, a short-term solution, since the bits of plastic could still be eaten by creatures or enter the ecosystem in tiny parts too small for a kid to pick up on the side of the road. Recently, a craft brewery has invented a six-pack ring made from barley and wheat that is completely edible by marine life, or at least by marine life who want to eat barley and wheat. I assume it's edible by human life too. An ad for the brewery explains that Americans drink 6.3 billion gallons of beer a year, and half of that beer comes in cans. Against a backdrop of a six-pack ring floating in blue water, the ad says, "Most of the plastic six-pack rings used end up in the ocean." I'm not sure where they get that "most," or how one would measure such a thing, but if I'm doing my arithmetic correctly, those rings strung together would be the length of 83,760,683 school buses or 65,333,333 humpback whales. This number seems impossible until I consider that you can buy 4,300 six-pack rings (made in the USA!) for 160 bucks.

What were not in those ditches—I know for sure—were plastic

T-shirt-style grocery bags. I was a junior in high school in 1987 the first time my mom came home from the store with plastic grocery bags. I remember looking at them lined up on the kitchen counter and thinking, "That looks like a bad idea." Each bag's translucent skin held only a few items—a carton of ice cream or a few cans of soup. At least you could cram a ton of stuff in a decent paper bag. Plastic T-shirt bags first appeared in American grocery stores in 1979, and even though 75 percent of stores had them available in 1985, only a quarter of customers preferred them. By 2003 four out of every five grocery bags were plastic. Today, of course, they are ubiquitous.

Songs of the Humpback Whale was kind of impossible to sing along with, so I also played various *Sesame Street* albums on our kiddie record player, including one featuring a song called "The Garden," which is not to be confused with "Garden Song," a cheerful melody about planting seeds John Denver performed on a 1979 episode of *The Muppet Show,* accompanied by a choir of oversized pansies, a prickly pear, and a watermelon, all flapping throat-less, wedge-shaped mouths. In "The Garden," on the other hand, Susan croons with Oscar the Grouch about litter, a dark moral lesson evoking a kid version of apocalypse. Susan warns that if we throw trash on the ground, pollute the air, and toss junk in the ocean, we'll regret it. It's prescient. She sings, "You take a lot of trash and dump it in the bottom of the sea. The octopuses and the oysters won't complain to you and me. But someday you might get hungry for a tuna fish fricassee, and you've got a glop glop grungy glub garden where the ocean used to be." Goodbye, sad humpback whales. The song ends with the ominous suggestion that you might end up with this mess "where the whole world used to be," a nightmare image of Earth as landfill that horrified me and scared me straight on littering.

Kids today do have global warming, but during the Trump administration they couldn't learn about it from the Environmental Protection Agency website. In May 2017, the EPA took down a page called "A Student's Guide to Global Climate Change" in order "to reflect EPA's priorities under the leadership of President Trump and Administrator Pruitt," as the website stated under a banner reading "The page is being updated."

NASA has a "Climate Kids" website, which goes into such things as arctic oscillation, a description of which features a photo of the Obama's puppy Bo enjoying deep snow. The site also discusses the choice between paper and plastic, concluding that both are bad for the environment and suggesting that one should bring one's own bag to the grocery store instead, though it says that the checkout clerk may forget to ask you, "Did you bring your own bag?" Fifteen years ago, I had to convince checkout clerks that I didn't need my groceries packed in plastic bags before they were put in my cloth bags, and just the other day a clerk insisted against my protests that she put some cleanser I'd bought into a plastic bag "so it wouldn't explode all over everything else," a phenomenon that has never once happened in all my shopping years. As I watch shoppers head to the parking lot with enormous nests of blue plastic bags in their carts, I want to travel to some of the places that have banned the use of the T-shirt bag, such as California, so I can see if it feels like 1979. Though the United States is cutting-edge about making stuff, we're behind on banning stuff.

Lots of countries, including China, have bans on using plastic bags or giving them away for free. In Kenya, trafficking in any way with plastic bags—making, selling, using—can get you a $40,000 fine or four years in jail, a sentence roughly equal to a quarter of the recommended lifespan of a school bus.

I'm curious what people are teaching second and third graders about the environment nowadays. As I search for lesson plans about climate change, I begin to think maybe it's a bit like nuclear annihilation—off limits until fourth or fifth grade.

What I find for the younger kids on the sites about climate change is a lot like my own Dos and Don'ts from forty years ago—pick up litter, turn off the lights, don't waste water, ride your bike. Some feature Dr. Seuss's book *The Lorax,* which was written in 1971. A new addition to the Dos is "Recycle paper, plastic, glass, and cans." My own childhood version of recycling meant my sister and me going around with a wagon collecting neighbors' newspapers so we could get some cash for them. Plastic water and soda bottles didn't exist back then, and neither did curbside recycling. Today, it turns out that just taking a school bus can help the environment, so that's a pretty easy thing for little kids to do, because each bus keeps an average of thirty-six cars off the road. But some of the lessons I find just leave me scratching my head. The NASA Climate Kids website suggests making an ocean ecosystem dessert out of blue Jell-O and Swedish Fish. And then—eat it? Maybe NASA should stick to educating us about things in space, like the school-bus-sized asteroid that buzzed between Earth and the moon in January 2017, a few days after President Trump's inauguration.

Dumping unsolvable problems on the kids who will inherit

them is unfair. Little kids are victims of damage, not perpetrators, though the United States does produce about 345 humpback whales' worth of disposable diaper garbage a day. Maybe included on the list should be "grow into the kind of person who cares, but who also acts on their concern." But that kind of growth would be hard to measure with school buses or humpback whales. Maybe the environmental Dos and Don'ts we share with kids only make us, the older generations, feel less guilt for our own complicity in the world's problems and our confusion about how to fix them. Somewhere between kidhood and adulthood, I forgot that the world wasn't always this injured. I've been witness and accomplice to destruction, which felt inevitable, because a lot of people do care and act, and still the situation is dire. We ask kids to believe something we don't really believe ourselves—that they can change the future. If we believed this, then we'd address the root cause for what it is—our own human weakness. One thing I remember about my Dos and Don'ts is that they felt like a battle cry against an outside danger, some evil force trying to ruin my planet, and strangely that made me feel like a solution might be possible.

Though not much seems to have changed in the environmental curriculum over the last decades, I consider one thing little kids do learn in school today that I was never taught: how to barricade themselves within their own classrooms while a "bad guy" roams their halls with a firearm. In one lesson, kids are taught to stack chairs and desks against the door in order to "make the classroom more like a fort." I find a photo of fifth graders crouched on the floor, holding their textbooks as though they might use them as shields. Another lesson teaches students to throw objects at the bad guy to distract him. One school recommended students keep canned goods in their desks for this very purpose. These lessons suggest that simply knowing and following the rules will save their lives. What the students aren't taught is that the bad guy is very likely to be one of them.

I'm about as old as the lifespan of a humpback whale. As an American, that means I'm probably responsible for around 89,500 pounds of garbage thus far, or 1.4 humpback whales. The nation produces 24,649 humpback whales of garbage each day, 8,996,923 per year. In its 250,000-mile lifespan, a school bus produces emissions, including half a baby humpback whale of carbon monoxide and 40.5 adult humpback whales of nitrogen oxides. A humpback whale produces nothing that damages the world it lives in. Instead, it contributes to this planet the longest, loudest, slowest dirge—its mournful songs.

the galápagos
shooting gallery

November 2010. The tourists step away from the plane and immediately rush over to the cactus. It's the first cactus available for backdrop, a person-high cactus of the prickly pear or opuntia variety. Two women pose while a man takes their picture. I've just arrived on Baltra, a flat slab of an island in the Galápagos a short ferry ride from Santa Cruz, where my Aunt Bec has been working as a volunteer at the Charles Darwin Research Station in Puerto Ayora. I hustle past the tourists to the queue for the hundred-dollar national park fee and baggage claim. I want to leave air travel behind and find my aunt and take the ferry. There will be other opportunities to be seen with opuntia.

I spent last night mostly not sleeping in the Quito, Ecuador, airport. At 12:45 a.m., when I got off my plane, I claimed one of the few remaining seats in the only area of the Aeropuerto Internacional Mariscal Sucre open all night, a chilly space outside the terminals about as big as a small big-box store. Among the Ecuadorians sleeping on seats who came prepared with blankets, I erected an encampment of suitcase and backpack, put on all of my available layers of clothing, and took out my laptop. With the webcam, I snapped a shot of myself at the beginning of my adventure, and in it I noticed wrinkles I didn't know I had.

A little over a month ago, the Ecuadorian Air Force took over the airport during a coup attempt to oust President Rafael Correa. I thought of this as we taxied in the morning, remembering the photo I'd seen of the troops lined up to block the runway. During the flight to Guayaquil and then the Galápagos Islands, the flight crew broadcast an endless video of some program involving people playing practical jokes on innocent bystanders, iterations of the same joke on different people. The jokes weren't mean, just foolish. The idea was to catch someone on video being confused or shocked, and then relieved when it's all revealed to be a joke. As other people on the plane laughed, I found myself embarrassed, ashamed to witness these small miseries. Before we landed, the flight crew handed us all empty souvenir Galápagos tote bags. I wondered what we might put in them.

Galápagos National Park has a list of rules meant to protect the delicate balance of life on the islands. It includes a catalog of things we are not to do, such as bring live material to or between the islands; touch, startle, or feed the animals; disturb nests; litter; deface rocks; wander away from designated visiting sites; buy souvenirs made from plants or animals of the islands; or take any plant, animal, or natural object from the islands. The final rule on the list: show your conservationist attitude.

In 1897 Californian ornithologist and specimen collector Rollo Beck joined an expedition to the Galápagos funded by the wealthy and somewhat eccentric Lord Lionel Walter Rothschild, who gathered animals, living and dead, from all over the world at his museum on his estate in England. Roaming the grounds were zebras, cassowaries, kangaroos, and kiwis, to name a few. In his teens, Rollo Beck had learned the art of animal preservation—that is, taxidermy—and had risen in the field, selling mounts to museums, making a name for himself as a collector of specimens. The purpose of the Galápagos expedition was to collect giant tortoises for Rothschild, which Beck did. Rothschild subsequently named one of the subspecies of tortoise Beck found *Testudo becki*. I come across a photo showing Rothschild, who was a husky six foot three, riding a giant tortoise, encouraging it with a bit of greens on a stick held out in front of its head. The tortoise apparently was an Aldabran tortoise, not a Galápagos tortoise.

A few hours after my arrival, my aunt gives me a tour of the research station, a compound of low buildings along the eastern lava shore of the island. Here is the home of Lonesome George, a poor tortoise who, as the last of the Pinta Island subspecies, has a celebrity status. He's the mascot of the station. He's also the name on a line of upscale clothing marketed to the islands' tourists. Doom sells. He lives in an outdoor complex housing the station's giant tortoise breeding and rearing program. More genetically successful tortoises plod around rocky corrals, scraping their way on round-bottomed feet. I'm inside an enclosure watching one the size of a bumper car watch me. A young blond woman with a German-sounding accent joins me and asks if I'll take a picture of her with the tortoise. She crouches down next to its scarred shell, smiles a practiced smile. She offers to take mine and, checking the result, frowns at my camera. "Let me take another," she says. "You look, I don't know the word—surprised?" Next to me, the tortoise shifts, the sandpapery rasping of several hundred pounds of reptile. Another tortoise lumbers over to us and lunges its monstrous head at the woman's bright yellow sneakers.

The next day, my aunt and I visit Rancho Primicias, a giant tortoise reserve on private land, where for a few dollars we can stroll unaccompanied around the landscape of grasses, shrubs, trees, and rocks. It's morning, and the tour buses haven't arrived yet, so there's no one in sight but the occasional finch. A few hundred feet away from the shack that serves as ticket office, cantina, and souvenir shop, we see a dark, shiny mound in a field of low grass. I take a picture from a distance, then move closer. The tortoise, indifferent, chews on a sprig of green hanging from its mouth. I squat down, aim my lens, and frame shots, closer and closer. The tortoise sucks in its neck, a hissing pneumatic sound, but I persist. Finally, I see under its shell, its head filling the frame, the knobby keel of its plastron bulging out beneath. The only things between its eye and mine are a few inches and the camera.

At the rancho, the tortoises turn out to be everywhere. At a small watering hole, we find eight hunkered in the muck. A man in a wheelchair aims a long telephoto. He's got a tripod and a bag full of equipment. My aunt and I position ourselves around the pond, careful not to get in the way of his pictures. Every so often, a tortoise will move in the water, lifting its head, stirring up the muddy pool. Flies buzz. The dry leaves of the trees rattle. The tortoises, when they chew, sound hollow. I wonder about tortoise time. They can live to be nearly two hundred years old, and their average lifespan is around one hundred. A tortoise in the pond decides to get out; it takes a while. Do they even register us, or are we blurs, circling them like gnats? Friends of the man join us. Now there are five of us surrounding the pond, our lenses protruding and drawing back in as we focus and zoom and try to get it all in.

In 1905 Beck led an expedition back to the Galápagos for the California Academy of Sciences on a schooner named *Academy*. Again, he collected tortoises, as well as sea turtles, lizards, snakes, plants, and birds. There's a photo of the team of eight men on the ship, taken, I'm guessing, before they left. They wear woolen suits, ties, and hats, and each seems to be staring off in a different direction. I've read the expedition notes, printed in a monograph by the Herpetologist's League, of one of the young men on the team, Joseph Slevin, a twenty-four-year-old herpetologist. On the way to the archipelago, heading toward the Mexican island of San Benedicto, Beck catches his first sea turtle of the trip, a loggerhead. They take its picture and then dissect it, recording measurements. Slevin writes, "Plenty of dark red blood which had a fishy smell," and then reports the temperature of the turtle and the temperature of the air. He begins to skin the animal but, interrupted by a bout of seasickness, has trouble finishing in a timely manner. In the end, the flesh rots, and Slevin has to clean the bones and keep only the skeleton, rather than preserve the skin.

I'm at Tortuga Bay, a beach and lagoon open to the public a few miles south of Puerto Ayora. There's almost no one else on the long stretch of fine white sand. Marine iguanas emerge from the cyan sea and crawl past, leaving decorative tracks—a line from their tails between alternating footprints. Little sandpiper-like birds run along the surf, too quick for me to get a good picture. Brown pelicans float around a periwinkle sky. Between the beach and the lagoon runs a path with the rocky lava shore on one side and an opuntia forest on the other. I'm on the path, trying to take a shot of a whimbrel poking between the rocks. It's hard to set the right aperture on the camera with the black lava sending confusing signals to the camera's brain. When I turn around to face the forest, right behind me, a great blue heron stands, wings outspread to dry in the sun, as though impersonating the tall cacti around it. In the shade of a nearby cluster of mangroves, dozens of marine iguanas rest, occasionally spraying salty fluid out of glands near their nostrils. They have no interest in moving out of the path. I'm alone, and so I hunker down with them, turn my camera to face me, and shoot. The sights are so like the photos in the guidebooks, I want proof that these images are my own, that I was the one who was here, not because I think no one will believe me but because I want to remember my being in this place, not just the place itself.

In late September 1905, nearly three months into their trip, the crew of the *Academy* finally reaches the island Española of the Galápagos. Beck goes ashore and takes some pictures. The next day, Slevin travels ashore to do some collecting. He collects two snakes, but "one is very badly shot, almost in half." In his notes on the expedition, *collecting* almost always means *shooting*. He collects a few marine iguanas as well, but only a few, because he has no barrels, no place to put them. Instead, he writes, he will "lay in a few skulls as soon as possible." Skulls take up less room. The group doesn't have much luck for a week or so, but then Slevin collects 125 geckos along a slope of the island. He writes about the difficulty of preserving the animals on the boat. With all of the rolling, he has trouble keeping the tails straight before they harden.

They stop on San Cristóbal and visit the settlement there. It's surrounded by cultivated fields, and Slevin guesses there won't be much to hunt in the area. Soon, they move on to Santa Cruz, where their collecting begins to pick up momentum. They find their first giant tortoises. They kill two females, but because it's getting too late in the day to kill and skin a male they've discovered, they flip him onto his back and lash his legs to a tree. When they return in the morning, he's gotten free but hasn't gone far. Like the females, he ends up, according to Slevin, "in pickle."

I try not to judge. These men thought that the creatures of Galápagos were about to die out. Beck himself had worried about their extinction after his first visit and spread his concern. An article I read about the expedition calls their activities "salvage collection," saving evidence of the species so scientists may study the animals many years after the creatures' inevitable disappearance. I've heard this argument, and it makes sense in some ways. What would I do? I've considered the paradox of preservation.

At the lagoon, I wade in and watch fish jumping from the water and, farther out, the heads of sea turtles periodically breaking the surface as they rise to breathe. I don't have a snorkel or mask, but I do have a small waterproof digital camera, which I stick below the surface. I click the shutter and capture nothing but an expanse of teal.

Walking back through Puerto Ayora to my aunt's apartment, I take pictures of the streets. Most of the buildings seem to be mid-construction. The ground floor might look like a perfectly complete stucco structure, but from its roof jut long spines of ribbed rebar, waiting for a second story. At one open-air shop, next to a display of shovels, an artificial Christmas tree teeters on the sidewalk, wrapped in orange garland. In a backyard, I spot an inflatable pool, a few clotheslines of laundry, some wooden pallets, a low wall of rocks, blooming bougainvillea, piles of bright pink impatiens, scattered cinder blocks, and a banana tree. Another house has a wall topped with wine bottles, their necks driven into the cement, a cheerful version of walls I've seen elsewhere topped with broken glass. I'm furtive with my camera, as there's clearly nothing scenic around, and I feel like what I am—someone looking too carefully at other people's lives.

Slevin's notes reflect a kind of intimacy with the animals. He blows their eggs, emptying the contents and measuring them. He systematically records the length of flippers, legs, necks, tails, bodies. He writes down what is in each stomach. He details the amount of fat on the flesh. He counts the eggs in the females' ovaries. When I read these statistics, I think of each animal as an individual, unique and worthy of his attention. I think about the two pieces of information that appear again and again in his entries: temperature of turtle, temperature of air. The turtle, a reptile, is almost always warmer than the air.

My aunt has signed us up for a cruise of the islands on a small catamaran carrying about two dozen people, including crew. On the first night we circle west around the southern side of the largest island, Isabela. As the sun rises, I watch constellations of blue-footed boobies hover and dive. I snap some pictures, but the still images don't reflect the suddenness of the birds' plunging, the way they float above the waves, then, in an instant, transform into missiles, diving directly into the sea. In the morning light, the birds in my pictures are curved dark wings against the gray water; they could just as well be crows or gulls anywhere in the world. Later we ride the inflatable Zodiacs the guides call pangas to the island to hike on lava fields where small lagoons create oases of green with fish and birds. At one spot, I take shot after shot of a trio of pink flamingos wading at the edge of a green pool. I frame and reframe the birds, the volcano in the distance, the black lava. Our group lingers awhile at the lagoon, pointing our cameras. The birds stand almost perfectly still. They look a little fake. I give up on flamingos—I've seen them before at the zoo. What I've never seen before are the frigatebirds, which bob like toy kites above the pond, then swoop in to catch fish. They aren't built to land on water, so when they strike the surface, they struggle to break free, loudly working their wings, shaking their V-shaped tails. Brown pelicans alight and drift in the pond. I shoot a few short video clips, but they're grainy, so the birds appear only as wide blades crashing into the water with a white splash. On the hike back to the shore, I take a picture of a deep crevasse in the lava, a crack to nowhere. In the photo, the chasm looks like a black line. In the last hour or so, I've tried 140 times to save what I've seen.

Two months into the *Academy*'s exploration of the Galápagos, as the crew collects on Pinzón, Slevin writes, "We have been here two weeks now and probably have about 80 tortoises." He tells of a sea turtle the men shot and decapitated, the body slipping away into the ocean before he could get any measurements.

From 1997 to 2002, I taught darkroom photography at a high school in Oregon. I loved the feel of the film in utter darkness as I unrolled it off its spool and onto the steel developing reel—the shushing as I slipped it around and around the wire coil. I loved the pickle smell of stop bath after the magical appearance of a print in developer. I had two cameras—a 1960s-era single-lens reflex Pentax Spotmatic and an even older medium-format twin-lens reflex Rolleiflex. I had an array of lenses—telephoto, zoom, wide-angle, fish-eye. I owned nothing digital. It didn't take long to shoot a roll of film, but I needed at least two hours to make that film into a finished picture.

In February 2001, my sister in California gave birth three months prematurely to my niece. Because I lived on the West Coast, I was at the hospital, reporting back to family in the Midwest. I took pictures of the tiny baby girl with my Pentax, not knowing how they'd turn out, then flew home to Portland, immediately developing the black and whites in the darkroom. I remember standing in the dark, closing the lid on the developing canister, hoping everything—*everything*—would turn out. When the prints were finally dry, I scanned them onto a computer. My niece appeared gray in the pictures, which didn't improve an already desperate-looking portrait cluttered with tubes and instruments. Using Photoshop, I added a tint of pale pink and emailed the file to her grandparents.

My waterproof camera is as small as a tin of breath mints. I tested it before the trip by taking a picture in my bathroom sink. It seemed to work. I got a good picture of a bathroom sink. This morning, we're going snorkeling off Punta Moreno on Isabela, and I'm armed. The water is around sixty-two degrees, which sounds, but is not, warm-ish. I'm wearing a short wetsuit and light blue flippers that make me look only slightly like a booby. Except in a swimming pool, I've never been snorkeling. When I hit the cold water, I can't breathe, huffing and huffing, but not filling my lungs. I clasp my camera tight to my chest, noticing for the first time that it doesn't have any sort of strap. When I can finally inhale through the snorkel's mouthpiece, I dip my mask into the ocean, testing it out, expecting to find the same stretch of empty water I saw from the panga. Instead, about six feet away, a huge green sea turtle swims around. The current pulls me toward it, and I can't figure out how to move in reverse, so I swim over the top of it as it passes below, a flat, finned boulder drifting weightless above rock and strands of seaweed. The camera remains in my clutching hand, unused. When the turtle is gone, I turn it on and start shooting. Now I know what I'm looking for.

A sea lion cruises past, its belly a few feet from my own. It torpedoes by so quickly it looks like a gray streak. Only later, when I examine my pictures on my computer, can I see the whiskers around its snout, its eye watching me. It makes a few passes, and I try to call to the other snorkelers, "Hey! Sea lion!" but through the mouthpiece it just sounds like a screech, my consonants sucked away. They'll have to find their own sea lion. I come across a pair of turtles dangling in the surf rushing off the lava shore. With their flippers waving, they seem to fly. One swims a foot or two from my lens. I put my hand in the frame, to place the turtle's great size against a reference, but the camera reads my hand as the subject to focus on. My hand, a few white fingers reaching, the turtle, a blurry disc in the background. The turtles seem like an idea on the edge of my mind, approaching clarity—startling, huge—then slipping back into the cloudy water.

In one entry of the expedition notes, Slevin writes that the crew's mate went to a lagoon to get more sea turtles but found them scarcer than usual. He mentions in several entries that they can't find tortoises in places Beck had seen them on his first voyage, that the people living on the islands tell them the animals are gone. At particular locations, he laments a lack of lava lizards or geckos. Beck comes across a hunting camp scattered with tortoise bones. About a stop on Santa Fé, Slevin writes: "Made another search for tortoise but find no live ones. Beck found some more bones on the higher portions of the north end of the island. He mentions yesterday having seen a very old piece of dung."

In addition to the dead specimens, they also keep a number of live tortoises on board, but some perish, either from injuries incurred during their capture or from illness. While Slevin is on a hunt for tortoises on San Salvador, two Española tortoises on *Academy* die and rot to the point of near uselessness. What was this boat like, with its skeletons, its skulls, its skins drying, its bodies soaking in preservative, its live specimens with their needs? Did the crew ever see any irony in their work, or at least feel a little uncertain, recognize any room for gray?

In the afternoon, we take the pangas to a large black rock covered in white guano jutting up from the ocean. We've been anchored near it for a few hours. As the pangas close in on the rock, our guide Daniel says, "Get your cameras ready," and only now do I see them, though they've been there all along—little penguins, about a foot tall, their black-and-white bodies now visible against the rock. We motor slowly around the islet, snapping photos of boobies and penguins, pelicans and iguanas. I'm trying to focus on one penguin standing on a big boulder when I turn around and find two young brown pelicans bobbing in the water within arm's reach, observing me.

We take the pangas on a slow tour of a mangrove lagoon, where quiet stretches of water loom between knobby mangroves, low and shady. Daniel tells us that in the mud at the bottom, sea turtles rest. At first we don't see any, but then we begin to make out the shape of their shells below. The driver shuts off the motor and Daniel paddles with an oar. My aunt uses a polarizing lens that cuts through the glare on the water's smooth surface. I lean over the side of the boat, holding my waterproof camera underwater as I click the shutter. I don't know what's before me until I look at the screen to check. Sometimes I have nothing but a landscape of wavy mud caught in bands of sunlight. But sometimes, the bulk of a turtle, disturbed by the boat, is shoving off from its dozing spot to rise for a breath.

On the boat in the evening, the frigatebirds dangle just overhead. Everyone gets out their cameras to take pictures, trying to steady themselves against the waves as they point their lenses to the sky. One of the birds shits in a young Canadian guy's beer. Later, I'm alone on the top deck watching the sun set over the island with the penguins, not another group of humans in sight on any horizon. I imagine the penguins in the darkness, indistinguishable from rock.

At night, I lie on a deck chair looking at the stars, unmarred by any manmade light. Soon, I'm joined by several other passengers from all over the world—Canada, the United Kingdom, Germany, Australia. They want to know which constellation is the Southern Cross. I have no idea. One of the guys has an iPhone with a constellation application. He tries to figure out how to make it work. Everyone passes around his iPhone, looking for the right set of stars to match the sky. No luck. Above us, dots hang in the black.

On April 3, 1906, Beck collects a single giant tortoise from a mountain on the island of Fernandina. He skins it on the spot and carries the shell down to the boat on his back. It is the only and last tortoise ever found on the island, its own subspecies, though they don't know it at the time.

A few months later, Slevin enters the information for another tortoise, writing, "This was a very old male; the plates on the side of the carapace were loose in life and plates on top all chipped up. The forelegs were scarred by the dogs and he was a regular old patriarch all around."

The next day at Urbina Bay, we stalk land iguanas, which are rust colored and shier than marine iguanas. We see Galápagos hawks and Galápagos doves, finches and flycatchers. We snorkel off the beach. I spend nearly a half hour swimming around, photographing the same sea turtle as it feeds off the rocks. It tolerates my company like it tolerates the company of the bright, foot-long fish that floats near its head, dodging at matter the turtle has dislodged. Again and again, I pop to the surface with the turtle as it rises to breathe, my elbow almost swiping its flipper, our movements synchronized. I study it, photo after photo—close-ups of head, eye, tail, shell. In the moment, the turtle means everything, it seems, and I have to preserve this connection, or what I perceive as connection. Eventually, my hands go numb from cold, and I can no longer hold the camera, and I swim toward shore, leaving the turtle behind.

At Punta Espinoza on Fernandina, I've moved beyond stills. The little waterproof camera takes nice video, it turns out, and I try to capture the locomotion of the animals—the brown hawksbill turtles swimming, the sea lions rolling around and fighting, the herons and pelicans and cormorants presiding on rocks, the iguanas snorting. I shoot a clip of dozens of green sea turtles floating in a shallow bay, an alien army drifting in the waves. I take pictures of my aunt taking pictures, her hand steadying her long lens, evidence of how close we really are to the animals. *We were right there—right there!*

In the late afternoon, the boat starts its journey northward, and off to the west, we spot the spouts of Bryde's whales. Everyone runs to the west side of the boat—those with cameras ready, clicking away. I don't have my camera. I have a cold beer instead. There are several whales, and the captain slows down the boat so we can stick with them awhile. They surface on the east side, and everyone stumbles across deck to see them, footing unsure on the rough water. The people with cameras try to guess where the whales will surface next, framing small sections of ocean. One woman cries, "My memory card is full!"

In August of 1906, on Isabela, toward the end of their journey, the *Academy* crew find a pasture filled with hundreds of tortoise skeletons, butchered by the islanders for oil. Slevin's entry seems to record horror—"hundreds of them!" But on the same hunting expedition, he tells of killing a tortoise to "get the liver for lunch." He relates how, then, while they're off searching for specimens, their guide cuts off one of the same tortoise's legs for his own meal. In the end, they can save only the skull.

Reading the expedition notes, I wonder about knowledge and sacrifice. It may be that the work of the expedition contributed to the world's understanding of these animals and helped stave off their extinction. I know this. Still, again and again and again the notes read: "Skinned tortoises." In all, in their attempt to save evidence of the species, the expedition collected over 260 of the giant reptiles.

I'm thinking about technology, about the camera. We seem to see mainly through the lens, through the display panel, through what we can keep. Before digital, I took pictures without knowing how they'd turn out. I knew they could be easily ruined. Despite my love of photography, I distrusted it to hold history. I recall the oft-told story of photographer Robert Capa, who risked his life to take pictures of the D-Day invasion of Normandy, but, as the story goes, due to a darkroom error at *LIFE* magazine, only eleven of the frames survived.

But I'm in the Galápagos, and despite the plea to "show your conservationist attitude," not everyone does. The place is fragile, the animals in danger. Shouldn't I try to save what I can? Several times a day, I've opened my laptop, uploaded my data, kept my fingers crossed that it would all make it back home. I'm like the Mars landers, recording, sending photos to Earth from an otherwise unbelievable place. Someday, I'll wear out, end transmissions, but for now, I keep going.

An 1899 article in the *Bulletin of the Cooper Ornithological Club* includes a photo of Rollo Beck preparing a mount of a Galápagos tortoise. The animal is rather small and stands on a worktable. Beck, in a dark vest and well-worn hat, holds an instrument to the animal's eye. The tortoise is one he brought from his first trip to the Galápagos to his home in California. The article tells the story: "The tortoise lived for almost a year after its arrival at Berryessa and seemed to thrive upon a diet of cactus and would in all probability have lived many years to enjoy the salubrious climate of the Santa Clara Valley had it not on an evil evening forgotten to draw in its head! A frost came, the tortoise was nipped in the bud, and we present a very natural picture of Mr. Beck putting the finishing touches to a really excellent pose of the tortoise."

I've taken over a thousand pictures in the last few days. To the east, a sea lion jumps in front of a caldera bathed in orange sunset. An enormous manta ray drifts by the side of the boat. A booby dives. I think to myself, if only I had a camera ready at all times to take this down so I could come back to it, so I could be here again. A device that would grab these things, sort through them, and line them up for me to revisit. Then I realize what I'm imagining is memory.

A few moments before the whales arrived, we were simply tourists on a boat enjoying the late afternoon light, but the whales have given us a sight to see, and now we are whale watchers. We have something to do, to take, something, even, to take apart—to frame and study, static and preserved. I hold my beer, watch the whales with all of my vision, the wide, peripheral world suddenly huge around me. Unfocused, I find whales surfacing all over, a flash of spout, then a black hump disappearing—the ocean again unknowable, capable of anything.

cage

I encounter them a few stalls down from the white ducks huddled in a spot of shade behind a tarp, past the speckled eels circling a blue plastic tub of water—the sparse amenities of the doomed. The market runs along one side of a street in the Old Quarter of Hà Nội, several blocks of vendors under tin roofs. Across the street stand more permanent buildings: a narrow café open to the sidewalk, where men sit on foot-high red plastic chairs reading the newspaper, and a temple flanked by two shops selling coffins and funeral wreaths. On the market side, nestled next to an aquarium merchant with tropical fish swimming in jars and luminous artificial plants displayed on a plank like a festive centerpiece, the cages teeter in towers, tremulous wire and bamboo. Some hang from the corrugated tin roof, skeletal bells with swing clappers—the birds inside ringing. Some catch the morning light on their thin bars, scattering sun.

A cage keeps a living thing in but doesn't keep the world out. The breeze, the rain, the noise, the cold and heat, the darkness and bright, the reach of man, the insects, the poisonous air—all these pass through the bars to the thing inside. The word "cage" comes from the Latin "cavea," itself a word for "cage," which makes me think there have always been cages. No one knows where the word "cagey" comes from.

87

My husband and I have been in Hà Nội for a day. Before that, we were on planes for twenty-four hours. And before that, I was home, in the United States, in North America, the continent where I'd lived my whole life and which I'd never left. I was sitting on my front porch, watching morning traffic pass by and reading the paper in the sun while cicadas rattled the sycamores.

At the bird stall, some of the cages are hidden by red fabric covers. Some of the cages possess ornately carved bases. One has a perch decorated with dragon heads. The finer bamboo cages have tiny white-and-blue ceramic dishes for seed and water, while the wire cages have plastic feeders. The wire cages rustle with feathers and beaks. One, the size of a milk crate, holds a dozen yellow-green parakeets. In each bamboo cage, a single bird, every kind unfamiliar to me, yet distinct. A bird with a black crest, red cheeks, a white belly. A green bird with a blue throat and a red mark on its head. A small grayish-green bird with a curved beak, a white spot around its eye. I've never seen birds like these in cages, or anywhere.

In a wire cage resting on the ground, a pair of bantam chickens, a cock and a hen. Next to the chickens, also in a wire cage, lies a listless white kitten. The kitten's cage is a bird cage, with a dish of water and a wooden dowel for a perch.

Birds are fragile. It's hard to find someone who will care for them properly, someone who can notice their needs, which is why I'd never left my continent before. For fifteen years, we've had birds. First a duck, then a quail, then more ducks, then chickens and more quail. When I look at the bantams in the cage at my feet, I imagine my own little rooster back home, his call much like the rooster outside our hotel window on Yên Thái.

Above the bantams sit several large wire cages full of dull brown birds. Unlike the birds in the bamboo cages, whistling tunefully, these birds cheep. Their feathers frazzle, dotted with droppings. They ricochet around, grasping the wires with their feet and then letting go. They look familiar. Unlike the other birds, which have seed, the only food these birds have is a pile of cooked rice on the bottom of their cage.

I'm wondering if I should be outraged by these birds at the bird stall—their conditions, their probable poaching, their expendability. As I stand there, a man scoops a small pile of the dead off the ground with a shovel. The temperature is a hundred degrees and rising. And yet, somehow, I'm elated by the birds—their precise beauty, their delicate homes, their graceful dishes of seed. When the din from the motorbikes in the street dies down, I can hear them singing.

After a few minutes, I figure out what the dull birds are. Sparrows. I know of recipes made with sparrows, and perhaps these may be for cooking. Now I think I understand the crowded cages, the rice. I only wonder about all the tiny bones.

"Sparrow" is the name of an Air Intercept Missile used by American forces. Originally designed for targets beyond visual range, Cold War threats hurtling toward the homeland, it was fired from planes and guided by radar to take down enemy aircraft. In the Vietnam War—or the American War, as it's called in Việt Nam—the Sparrow wasn't really used this way because of concerns about Identification Friend or Foe protocol. Instead, pilots had to know who they were shooting before firing. In the end, its "kill probability" during the war was considered disappointing. This language surrounding the Sparrow feels resistant, an obstacle I can't quite cross. I've never seen a Sparrow missile in real life, but in the labeled pictures, the Sparrow is a long tube with a cone on one end, four wings in the middle, and four fins at the end. The difference between wings and fins appears imperceptible. To me, they all look like wings.

Depending on who's telling the story, the names change. Sometimes it's a story about South Vietnam versus North Vietnam and the Vietcong. Sometimes it's a story about the People's Army of Việt Nam and the National Front for the Liberation of South Việt Nam versus the American-supported puppet regime. Sometimes it's a story about the American military and the Army of the Republic of Việt Nam versus the Việt Cộng and the communist North. These names are all variants of *us* and *them*.

At the bird stall taking pictures, I'm a tourist. This is what I do—record what I see so I can process it later. I want to research these birds, find out what they are, put a name to something mysterious. Surely there's a book out there somewhere with these birds in it, neatly marked with a list of facts. I move from cage to cage, the camera finding the focus. Only after the woman running the stall grabs my wrist, shaking her head angrily at my camera, do I remember that this is someone's life I'm standing in. If I could speak the language, I could tell her I just enjoy the birds and want to keep a memory of them with me. Instead, I must seem nosy and judgmental, or simply in the way. I feel ashamed or sad or both, a confusion that grows later when I look at my photos and notice in them something I'd missed: a small Vietnamese boy, crouched down, taking pictures of the kitten.

In a neighborhood south of the market lies Hỏa Lò prison, built by the French in the 1880s to house Vietnamese prisoners and known later to American prisoners of war by the nickname Hanoi Hilton. I've heard stories of torture and inhumane conditions and executions from when the French ran the prison, and I've heard stories of torture and inhumane conditions and executions from when the Vietnamese ran the prison. One of its more famous prisoners was US senator and 2008 presidential candidate John McCain, who was captured after his plane crashed into a lake in Hà Nội. Another prisoner was Joseph Kittinger, the man who once held the record for the highest, fastest skydive. Today, much of the prison is gone, destroyed to make way for new construction. What's left is now a museum, which I don't visit. It isn't something I feel I need to see, just like the preserved body of Hồ Chí Minh at the mausoleum complex, which I also skip. Both of these are on my guidebook map, along with the Temple of Literature, which I do visit, and something simply labeled "Paddleboats," which I don't.

Back home, when we'd lose one of our birds to predators, we'd devise new ways of keeping them safe. For nearly eight years, we carried a much-loved pet duck inside each night to sleep in a tub in our basement. She died while we were on a trip away, when the boy watching her failed to get her in before dark. Something chewed her head completely off, leaving no trace, though her body was perfectly intact. We once built what we thought was a secure cage for a few dozen bobwhite quail we'd raised from eggs to release. One night, a raccoon reached in and killed six or seven, pulling parts of their bodies through the chicken wire. We've also lost chickens to hawks that flew into the yard and hen house. I came home once to find a bantam hen being eaten alive, the hawk pulling off breast meat as she still breathed. Each time, I thought maybe if I had done this or that to protect them, they wouldn't have died.

I've also heard stories of torture by the South Vietnamese, overseen by American soldiers, using methods American forces taught them. One story that's difficult to deny is of the Côn Sơn Island "tiger cages" off the coast of Việt Nam at the site of a former French prison. Here men and women—suspected communists, people who protested against the government and war—were kept in five-foot-by-nine-foot cells with bars on the ceiling, three to five prisoners to a cell. Before the cages were discovered and revealed to the world by two visiting US congressmen, the chief American adviser on Vietnamese law enforcement and prison techniques, Frank E. Walton, a former deputy chief of the Los Angeles Police Department and regular visitor to the prison, had compared Côn Son to a "Boy Scout recreational camp." After the revelation, he said, "You aren't supposed to go poking your nose into doors that aren't your business." Prisoners of the cages tell stories of drinking their own urine, of having lime dumped on their bodies, of eating rice mixed with sand. Photographs published in *LIFE* magazine in July 1970 taken by the aide of the visiting congressmen show both of the politicians standing over openings in the floor and emaciated prisoners staring up through the bars. The bars are bright stripes, out of focus in the foreground.

The Vietnamese language is tonal, each word carrying six potential meanings depending on the pitch—mid-level, low falling, low rising, high rising, low broken, and high broken. When I first heard Vietnamese being spoken in a film many years ago, the tones reminded me of birdsong, lilting and musical compared to the clacking string of consonants in English words. I tried to learn some Vietnamese before traveling, listening to hours of lessons on my commute to work, speaking aloud the words in my car, chatting with the scripted, recorded voice. Each lesson began with a conversation between two parties, which I was supposed to simply listen to with no expectation of comprehension. Then the lesson took apart the conversation so I could learn the pieces, begin to recognize them in context. The lessons would present scenarios: "Now suppose you are an older man, speaking with an older woman, how would you say 'hello' to her?" And I'd try to imagine myself an older man in a place I'd never been and say aloud, "Chào bà."

My father, an American veteran of the war, suspects that many Vietnamese people disappeared after the end of the war. This is the word he uses, *disappeared,* a term sometimes paired with "were" in the passive construction "were disappeared," which really means "were executed." No one I meet in Việt Nam speaks of this. And I would never ask. I think of the United States, my nation—a nation with the world's highest documented incarceration rate, a nation that actually holds more people in prison than any other in the world, a nation that keeps around 45,000 children detained each day, a nation that has executed over 1,500 of its incarcerated citizens since 1976.

When you put something in a cage, it becomes your responsibility. The burden of being caged is on the caged. The burden of the cage is on you.

On March 1, 1972, flying an F-4D Phantom over the mountains of Laos, Joseph Kittinger shot down a MiG fighter plane in air combat using Sparrow missiles. Two months later, he was shot down by the People's Army of Việt Nam and held prisoner for eleven months in Hòa Lò. Before this, in the late sixties, when my father was stationed in Germany, he met Joe Kittinger, whom he described as a quiet, unassuming guy. At first, my father told me, the young special forces officers in Bad Tölz didn't know who Kittinger was, and they razzed the older man a little, thinking he was a "leg," which is, as my father would put it, "a soldier who doesn't jump out of perfectly good airplanes." Then someone found his name in the record books, longest parachute free fall—over sixteen miles in four and a half minutes. Skydiving, he'd approached the speed of sound. In a single jump, my father thinks, Kittinger had probably fallen farther and longer than most of those young officers had in their careers so far.

The recorded voice says, "Ask the older woman, 'Do you speak English?'" Then silence as it waits for my question: Bà có nói tiếng Anh không?

The deaths of my birds troubled me but also strangely eased my worries. Eventually the quail all disappeared or died. The ducks flew away, living a semiwild existence, refusing, for the most part, to be protected by my measures. The chickens live in a wire-enclosed fortress, have a house with latches and locks. When they occasionally escape, they linger around the outside edge looking confused and can easily be corralled back. While I'd like to think my efforts aren't futile, I've also come to realize I can only keep so much at bay.

When John McCain ran for president in 2008, a group of veterans named Vietnam Veterans Against John McCain claimed he cooperated with the enemy in Hỏa Lò. They called him "Songbird." Though I find no reason to believe this, I'm never sure what to believe, except that the whole story isn't ever told. Or if it is, no one listens. Or if someone listens, they misunderstand. When I watch the 1967 film made by a French journalist of McCain as a wounded prisoner in a Hà Nội hospital, I see this: a man lying in bed, head propped on a pillow, smoking a cigarette. His voice on the film is sometimes obscured by the voice of the interpreter, speaking French. When the interviewer asks about the food, McCain jokes that the food isn't like the food in Paris, but that he still eats it. He has the look of a man remembering something, a man about to cry.

The phrase "một ít," pronounced with a low broken tone, means "a little." The older woman on the recording tells me she speaks English a little.

My father learned some Vietnamese when he was in the military, during his second tour as an officer, through the Army Special Warfare School in the late 1960s, first at Fort Bragg and then at Fort Bliss. He tells me stories of practicing his pronunciation while wearing headphones, of a Vietnamese female instructor who spoke only Vietnamese in class. While he was in language school, he was also in Army Special Warfare training to prepare to be part of the Phoenix Program, an operation overseen by the CIA that aimed to destroy the infrastructure of the Việt Cộng. When I ask him what he did in those classes, he says, "It's kind of hard to explain. I don't know whether I can explain it." He sighs and says, "You know, frankly, a lot of that period draws a blank for me."

On my return from Việt Nam, I watch a recording of a Vietnamese film shown to tourists at Hỏa Lò prison museum about the treatment of prisoners. At first it seems clumsy, like a parody of a propaganda film. A clip of prisoners sweeping the grounds with whisk brushes contains the caption, "The American pilots [*sic*] prisoners were taught to do things that every single Vietnamese child knows well how to do." It describes the prisoners as now having "the time and opportunity to learn more about 'their enemy,' whom they did not know very well before." The film shows a prisoner playing pool, a prisoner adding a whole pineapple to a full tray of food, a prisoner enjoying a water pipe. Then the film turns, oddly, to a series of shots of prisoners smoking cigarettes cut with shots of bombed-out Hà Nội, of Vietnamese bearing a coffin, of an injured woman being carried on a stretcher. In this segment, there are no captions.

My father isn't sure why he was chosen for language school. He'd never learned a language. He'd begun taking German classes while stationed in Germany, but he was an athletic guy in his twenties, and the classes were at night, and it was ski season, so he went skiing instead. He passed the army language aptitude test by one point.

The older woman now asks me, an older man, "Ông có nói tiếng Việt không?" *Do you speak Vietnamese?* I'm instructed to pay attention to the tones and reply, "Một ít tiếng Việt." *A little Vietnamese.* I'm comfortable with the phrase "một ít." It's easy. Unlike the word "ba," which has a tone I can't quite master. I may be saying "you" to an older woman. But I also might be saying "three" or "surround with one's arms" or "residue" or "poison."

What we don't see in the film of John McCain is a Vietnamese prison commander watching the scene. We don't see McCain's broken arm, which a doctor has been trying unsuccessfully to set without anesthesia right before the interview. We don't see anything below his shoulders. What we know is only what he tells the interviewer—that he's "treated well here," which isn't much, and may or may not be true.

My father explains the Phoenix Program like this: the goal was to identify the covert Việt Cộng government, to determine who these people were and "neutralize them." "Ideally," he tells me, "you didn't want to kill them." This is how my father tells some stories about the war, encircling them with language that only partially obscures. He tells me about priorities. The first priority was to recruit them, then send them back to gather information on the VC. "That," he tells me, "was pretty tricky" and didn't work out very often. The second priority was to capture them and convince them to defect. These people, he says, were put in a camp to protect them, but also to make sure they really would defect. The third priority was to capture them and hand them over to the South Vietnamese. The fourth priority was to ambush or assassinate them. The articles I read about the Phoenix Program either praise its effectiveness or, more often, condemn its reliance on the third and fourth priorities. My father's stories fall somewhere in between. He tells about the infrastructure the military repaired that had been ruined by war, about the civil engineering projects he supervised. He tells me the Vietnamese are good people.

I love birds but am a second-rate birder. I forget markings as soon as the bird disappears back into branches or sky. I know only a handful of songs or calls of the most ordinary birds. They pass through my brain, and I can't hold them.

In a 1973 *U.S. News and World Report* account of the hospital filming, McCain describes the commander, the broken arm. He doesn't share much more about the moment, except that the French journalist was a communist. In the same article, he writes, "As far as this business of solitary confinement goes—the most important thing for survival is communication with someone, even if it's only a wave or wink, a tap on the wall, or to have a guy put his thumb up. It makes all the difference." He also often uses a slur for the North Vietnamese and writes that "a lot" of the guards were homosexual. I try not to let this get in the way of my understanding, or maybe I am trying to understand this.

I come to Việt Nam knowing how to say only one thing very well, which is "Tôi nói tiếng Việt, không khá lắm"—*I don't speak Vietnamese very well.* Or literally, *I speak Vietnamese, not very well.* In Việt Nam, I practice this phrase on various tour guides, who repeat it back to me, kindly correcting my pronunciation.

If you put something in a cage, the caged thing transforms into your other, and you into its other. The cage stands between, though on unequal terms.

I ask my father what happened to the prisoners handed over to the South Vietnamese. He tells me he'd observed the interrogations. When I ask what they were like, he's unable to describe them. He says, "They weren't very nice." He says he made complaints, because he felt if the prisoners weren't Việt Cộng before the interrogations, they probably would be afterward. From our conversation, I sense he wants to believe that this kind of cruelty is unique to particular cultures; I want to believe that he doesn't truly believe this, given the evidence of our own nation's history.

My phrasebook includes the Vietnamese word for "bird"—"con chim"—and explains that "con" can be used as a classifier with the names of animals or, pejoratively, people. "Con" can also mean both son and daughter. Vietnamese for "song" is "bài hát." The phrasebook doesn't contain the word for "cage."

Although I feel certain the mysterious birds in the bamboo cages are exotic, whatever that means exactly, they aren't. They're common birds in Southeast Asia—the red-whiskered bulbul, the gold-fronted leafbird, the Japanese white-eye. The leafbird is a mimic. As it turns out, the white-eye, introduced to Oahu in 1929, is one of the most common birds on the Hawaiian Islands, and a small population of bulbuls lives in Florida.

I ask my father if he used his Vietnamese much during his time with the Phoenix Program. He says not really, that he felt more comfortable using an interpreter because there was "less chance of misunderstanding." But he also says it was good to have enough Vietnamese to know if the interpreter had skewed what he'd said.

I imagine myself as a younger man speaking to a younger woman: Chào chị. *Hello.* Chị có hiểu không? *Do you understand?* The younger woman is the wife of a Việt Cộng guerilla leader, who isn't at home when I visit her in the village. We're having tea. Tôi nói tiếng Việt, không khá lắm, so I use my interpreter. We're discussing her husband, how we might be able to get him to defect. Through the interpreter, she tells me it's unlikely, because even when he's in the house, he's never alone, there's always someone watching him. Another day, I'm in the village and she runs out to my jeep. Her baby is very sick, and she needs someone to get her into the hospital. Tôi hiểu. *I understand.* I have a baby daughter back home. So they climb in my jeep, and I take them to the hospital, make sure the baby gets care. I imagine myself as a younger man, a man who tells this story, a man who is my father. Afterward, my father explains, he wondered what would happen if he went to her house and her husband were there. What would the man do to the American who saved his baby? He never found out. One day, after an ambush, my father was the one who identified the man's body.

In Southeast Asia, some Buddhists practice the ritual release of birds. Birds can be purchased and then freed in a symbolic act of compassion. The popularity of the practice has led to problems. Birds are captured in large numbers and kept in small cages, transported far from their homes. Sometimes, when released, they are too weak to fly. I've heard stories of temple grounds dotted with dead birds.

One description of Hỏa Lò prison in 1914 tells of letters, presumably tossed over by Vietnamese prisoners, littering the pavement outside the wall.

When my father was in Việt Nam, he sent my mother cassette tapes he'd made, and she sent tapes back to him. I remember seeing the tapes when I was little. I never listened to them, nor have I ever asked what was on them.

In the lessons, I learn to say "I'm not Vietnamese." This isn't a phrase I ever need to use, and I quickly forget it. If anything is perfectly clear to anyone here, it's that I'm not Vietnamese.

Maybe I'm drawn to the bird stall because it has nothing to do with me. I can't buy the birds, so no one tries to sell me any— unlike the branches of spiky red rambutans, the long baguettes, the hats with the red stars, the rides on motorbikes I'm constantly being offered. The birds have nothing to do with America, with obligation, with perspective, with translation. The caged birds are about the people of Hà Nội, their pleasures. Through the birds, I try to see a world without me, and by seeing that world, I can perhaps better understand Việt Nam, despite my presence.

From Hà Nội, we take a tour to Hạ Long Bay, where we'll spend two nights on a boat. The tour van stops en route at a place the tour guide calls a "tour stop." It's a center for people with disabilities, who learn skills like sewing and embroidery. In a large workshop, fifty or sixty children lean over panels of fabric, embroidering elaborate scenes they copy from cards. Big fans move the air around the room. Most of the children have their shoes off and their feet resting on stools. The children look like they're in their early teens, maybe, or younger. Next to one girl's workspace is a paper fan decorated with pink princesses. Signs around the room tell us no photography is allowed. The children work on one side of the room, while on the other, tourists sit at tables eating snacks from the snack bar. One child wears a leg brace, but it's hard to tell what the other kids' disabilities are as they stitch quietly away with their needles and skeins of bright thread. Then a woman, one of the tourists, comes over to the workspace. She begins to shape the air with her hands—sign language—and dozens of the children look up, watch her, surprised. Then all of their hands are moving at once as they sign back, responding to the woman—a silent cacophony. They're smiling, and I wish I knew how to say something, anything, to them, like the woman reaching effortlessly across this barrier. On my way out, I buy some postcards and stamps, and a man who looks my father's age adds up the bill using a pen strapped to his upper left arm, which ends in a scarred stub. His right arm is missing entirely.

A bird in a cage is a common sight here, like the little plastic stools everyone sits on on the sidewalk or the wall-mounted fans in restaurants and shops. Cages dangle under awnings outside businesses, on the balconies of apartments, from trellises in the park. I see few lanterns but many cages. For the most part, the birds are songbirds. Their songs are hopelessly cheerful, as though they can say only nice things. In places around Hà Nội, I notice clusters of hanging cages, the birds inside brought together to sing to one another, which they do. What passes through the bars—a few shared notes, a gesture, a bit of seed—makes all the difference.

zoo world

The snake farm smells like a snake farm. I suppose it must look like a snake farm too, because that's what it is, or that's what we've been told it is. Our tickets say Trại Rắn Đồng Tâm and feature two cobras facing off on green grass. One cobra has a white blossom resting against it, as though it were the girl cobra and the other the boy cobra, and they're having a romantic conversation. It may even be a girl cobra, for all I know. The ticket costs twenty thousand Vietnamese đồng, or about one US dollar.

Really, the snake farm looks like a zoo. Tidy sidewalks bordered in grass lead visitors around the grounds, past rows of concrete cages not much bigger than dormitory refrigerators holding snakes, into buildings with more cages and even bigger snakes, to larger concrete enclosures with animals of nonsnake varieties, and by open air cages of more animals that aren't snakes. It's not a farm in the sense of the pepper plantation my husband and I visited a week before, which was pretty much peppercorn plants growing on posts and a small stand where we bought a few containers of extra-tasty black pepper. Here at the snake farm you can buy snakes—cooked at a restaurant on the grounds—but we've arrived late in the day and everything not in a cage is closing or closed, including the museum with dead snakes in tanks and the attraction where you can take your picture with a live python.

We have only about forty minutes to tour the place, so before someone comes along and locks the doors, we first visit the buildings with big snakes. Inside: elevated cages painted blue. Inside the cages: pythons. Big pythons, thick as a sturdy tree limb. Coiled up on the wooden slat floor of the cages, they don't move. Their skin glistens in the faint sunlight coming through the windows. I put my hand on top of a cage. The snake does nothing. The pythons, while huge and impressive, don't invite watching. The attraction of watching a python is considering what would happen if the python escaped. The cages have doors, and the doors have padlocks.

Outside, we head past a large octagonal tank with murky water about a foot deep where an enormous softshell turtle nudges against the glass. Nearby, a series of dirt-floored pens hold crocodiles lounging with their meaty legs splayed, feet pad-side up, as though lying in the dirt were exhausting. In one pen, a soft-drink bottle and snack chip bag rest near a croc. Farther along the path, a sun bear rolls around on the concrete floor of a small chain-link cage.

The nonsnakes capture my attention more than the snakes do. Why are they here? Trại Rắn Đồng Tâm is a military research facility. In addition to being a snake farm, it's a hospital treating snakebite victims from around the Mekong Delta. The promotional video for the farm shows groups of smiling tourists getting their photos taken while a python draped around their necks resists strangling them. The video also shows stricken locals lying on bamboo mats having their arms injected with antivenom serums and their wounds cleaned. Some pictures show shiny test tubes of yellowish liquid. Others show tourists pointing at snakes and nonsnakes. Still others show a machine pumping out snake-related products, such as Cobratoxan, an analgesic skin cream whose active ingredient is cobra venom—you can buy it on Amazon.

One sequence near the end shows tourists contemplating snakeskin belts and handbags. Footage of the actual snakes is limited, with the same clips cut in several times, one featuring a noble king cobra risen up from clipped grass, his head in profile.

Along the stretch of path with the dorm-fridge concrete cages, small cobras and other snakes stare out through wire mesh doors. I could stick my pinky finger through the mesh, which would be stupid. Inside the units, concrete shelves and fake rocks form little caves for the snakes to snooze in. Flowered dishes of water sit near the doors. The snakes lurk in various states of visibility, hunkered in the dark or peering at me as I crouch before them, their snaky odor dark and intense.

Time is running out, and the grounds of the farm are nearly abandoned. We pass a water monitor, some leopard cats, and what appears to be a river otter nibbling on a chunk of raw fish at the edge of a concrete pool full of brown water. We pass various primates in cages and a Sambar deer. We pass a bearcat. We pass an ostrich pecking at the chain-link fence of its enclosure and a peacock with only two short eye feathers left on its tail. We pass a pygmy slow loris. We pass something labeled "ratufa bicolor" that really isn't *Ratufa bicolor,* the black giant squirrel. Instead, it appears to be a fox squirrel, the sort common on my front lawn at home in Ohio. We pass some guinea pigs. We pass under a red metal triangular box lodged in the branches of a tree. A chain leads from the box to a monkey who perches in the tree, chattering.

It's closing time, so we head to the exit, where the stands selling snakeskin-this and snakeskin-that are all closed. The wide drive leading to the snake farm is full of kids kicking around balls. Our taxi driver, who also brought us here, has been waiting for us, so we get in the car, and he takes us to a restaurant on a boat in the city of Mỹ Tho. We don't want to go to the restaurant, but there doesn't seem to be any choice—it's part of the snake-farm-tour experience. So we order beer and snacks while he waits again for us in the parking lot, sleeping. Then he drives us back to our hotel in the town of Bến Tre, where we bike along the roads in the evening, past children playing and men sitting in front of houses along the river, drinking, who wave and call out, laughing, as we ride by, "Ello! Ello!"

I can't quite figure out how to get in the gate of the Yangon Zoo. Guards keep pointing me places, but I misinterpret their gestures, going to the wrong window, trying the wrong turnstile. Clouds loom, monsoon heavy. After several misstarts, I'm inside, having paid my foreigner entrance fee of about two dollars, and am following a road lined with trees and tropical plantings, punctuated by clusters of cages. The first cages hold birds—a hornbill, a silver pheasant, and a vulture called a Himalayan griffon. This species of griffon can have a wingspan of over eight feet, but the four griffons perched in the cage aren't showing off their wingspan as they fuss away, preening their feathers. Near the griffons, I spot a yellow slide and metal jungle gym—for human children, I assume.

It begins to rain lightly, and the rain travels to the drains in the sidewalk along the front of the bird cages. One of the grates on the drains has been slid off, leaving an opening big enough for people to fall through if they are too busy looking at birds to pay attention to their footing.

Farther down the path, two large cages hold a hoolock gibbon and a dusky leaf monkey, both species that can be found in Myanmar. The cages are chain link with weave large enough that I could slip my hand through if I wanted to, which I sort of do want to do, especially since the zoo is practically deserted and not one person is watching. Tires hang from ropes in the cage. The gibbon swings along the chain link to where I stand, and we stare at one another for a while. The bathrooms (for people) sit near the rear of the gibbon's cage, so I wander back to take advantage of the facilities, passing by the window where one would normally pay an attendant for use, but no one is there. Squatting inside the dark stall, I can hear it start to rain in earnest. Out on the path, a trio of monks walks by wearing rust-colored robes, carrying their brown umbrellas.

I follow the path up a hill to the deer displays, where dozens of deer loiter around several muddy, tree-shaded enclosures. Some of the deer are Eld's deer, an endangered species native to Myanmar, which the zoo breeds. A dozen deer hang out underneath the tin roof of a pentagonal shelter built over what appears to be a watering trough. The deer stand around and on the trough. Under another similar structure, a deer sits in the trough, as though relaxing in a hot tub. Elsewhere, a peacock wanders around one of the yards, as do some handsome roosters, which are anything but endangered in Myanmar.

The red panda exhibit features branches the panda can climb around on, which it does, friskily, a furry flash, running from an outdoor section to a roofed indoor section. The bars to the outdoor section are wide, and again I consider what would happen if I thrust my hand in to touch the panda, who is well within reach. The panda seems like it can't decide where it wants to be, running back and forth, and it makes me feel a little indecisive too.

All along the paths sit tented booths, some empty, some occupied by men and women staring out at the downpour, not bothering to cajole me into buying anything. The booths sell overripe bananas. I realize, seeing the bananas, that they're for feeding to the animals, and it would've been okay to stick my hand through the gibbon's chain link and perhaps even the red panda's bars. Or maybe, if I were holding a banana, the animals would reach through the bars to me. On a sunny, nonmonsoon day, I imagine lots of children offering fruit or vegetables to the deer and monkeys and hippopotami. I know on nice days the zoo staff take sun bears and other animals out of the cages to interact with visitors. Here and there throughout the zoo, fountains appear, shaped like cartoon creatures—a bunny, a penguin, a strange duckling with arms instead of wings. Pipes with spigots run from the animals' necks, tracheotomy-like, and buckets wait below. I wonder if these are for giving the animals water when they're wandering about in the hot sun. But today, the zoo is ruthlessly unsunny. I head to the elephants.

Rain falls in slabs. Dotted along the path are picnic tables with little roofs, and so I duck under one to arrange my raincoat over my backpack, protecting my camera. I'm soaked. I dart from picnic table to picnic table. A few picnic tables have young couples waiting out the rain, flirting, but otherwise, no one is around. Now, even the vendors have abandoned their stands. I make it to a small, covered stage area near the elephants, where I linger for ten minutes with a damp stray cat, looking out at a pavilion where it seems the elephants put on performances when it's not monsoon season. Beyond the pavilion, a concrete platform with a roof held up by columns, where the elephants stay. I make a break for it and splash through the puddles.

The zoo's elephants are what remain of the herd after many of the animals were moved in 2008 to a new zoo in Naypyidaw, where the military government relocated the country's capital in 2006. Several are shackled to the ground by yard-long chains. The rain pounds their roof, and they shuffle around, swinging their trunks, twitching their flappy ears. I'm wishing I had thick skin.

When the zoo opened as the Queen Victoria Memorial Park in 1906, one of its star attractions was a white elephant that had belonged to the last king of Burma, who had been living without his elephant for twenty years in India, where the British had exiled him. A white elephant is an auspicious symbol for Buddhists, auguring good fortune for a country. Even now, the government actively searches for white elephants and keeps a few they've found at a pagoda in Yangon, where they wait for visitors while chained on a platform like the one at the zoo but with a much more decorative roof. In 2013 the Thai government asked to borrow a white elephant as a symbol of the sixty-fifth anniversary of the two countries' diplomatic relations. Myanmar said no, and suggested, instead, that Thailand lend Myanmar some tourists to visit the elephants in Yangon.

I can't stand in the downpour forever, so I try to find some part of the zoo that has a decent roof for people to shelter under. As I wade down the path, I notice someone waving to me, calling. A woman at a booth, her wares covered in plastic tarps. She huddles behind her counter with her young son. I stop, and she scurries out to untarp her shelves, holding up what is, beyond any doubt, the ugliest umbrella in the world. She kindly opens it to show me its full horror. The canopy is patterned in red, black, gray, and light green with what appear to be faces of wide-eyed, mascaraed women emerging from either bowling pins or Shmoos. The edge is trimmed in red ruffles. I ask how much. Three dollars. I ask if she has any other umbrellas, but she's got only one other, which is smaller, flimsier, and nearly as ugly—royal blue, covered with pink hearts and smiley faces. I need coverage. I buy the ugly umbrella, thanking the woman, and set out toward the lions.

I think of the women I've seen in Myanmar with graceful lon-gyi sarongs, vividly patterned silks and cottons. I wear soaking wet gray travel shorts and carry the world's ugliest umbrella. I move from cage to cage, trying not to frighten the animals.

When I visit zoos, I feel like I'm looking through the cages at a mirror, at a reflection of humanity's own situation, at the conditions in which the zoos exist. A visit to a zoo forces me to think more carefully about what's outside the zoo. Zoos pry open the question of our own absurd dominion. I find myself thinking, "Are we—am I—really in charge? Who made that silly decision? Is my behavior any more responsible than the pygmy slow loris's?"

At the zoo in Loja, Ecuador, behind chain link, in a spacious, sunken concrete pit about twenty feet deep, a single male peacock displays his luminous tail. He struts around below, undangerous. Across the zoo, in a smaller, ground-level, grassy enclosure, also surrounded by chain link, a rusty sliding bolt latch secures a door: beyond the door, a napping puma. It's high noon at latitude 3.9° south, the sun beating down. I've paid my seventy-five-cent entrance fee to see the oso anteojos, or spectacled bear. Earlier in the day, I'd visited nearby Parque Podocarpus hoping I might glimpse the shy animal in the wild, but a landslide had washed away the road to the park's ranger station the day before, cutting off the trails. The zoo's single oso anteojos huddles in a strip of shade, about as wide as he is, beside a concrete wall painted with a mural of mountains. The noon sun renders the yard almost shadowless. I take a picture of the bear, zooming in so you can't tell he's in a zoo, his nose poking over tall grass, as though he can smell me. Above, in the wash of sky, Andean condors circle—their ten-foot wingspans, hovering silhouettes.

Squirrel monkeys race around an island in the middle of a shallow pond, climb in and out of elevated houses, and hunker in the grass. In a concrete cage, a black agouti guards a pile of cassava. The zoo workers, moving their weed whackers over the grass, are the only people around, except for a young couple wearing business casual, who seem to have taken off work for a lunch at the zoo, and a mother with a bunch of kids in tow. A large Galápagos tortoise shares a pen with a few deer, and I wonder what he thinks of his penmates, as there are no deer on the Galápagos. The only native mammals on land are the sea lions and fur seals, the rice rat, and bats.

Though there aren't deer on the Galápagos, there are other ruminants: goats. Introduced by man, these goats have done extensive damage to the ecosystem and the habitat of the tortoises, so much so that they've been the targets of an aggressive eradication campaign involving helicopters and sharpshooters, among other things. On San Cristóbal, an island that once held a penal colony, I've seen two of the estimated remaining three thousand goats who've escaped elimination thus far, nimble and determined, scaling the rocky northern hills.

Near the tortoise and deer display, a glass-faced building holds smaller, piggy-bank-sized tortoises and iguanas and also turquoise trash bins, like the kind found in a powder room, full of dirt and planted with flora and upturned plastic water bottles, I assume to maintain humidity.

Attached to one end of the zoo lies a greenhouse with an orchid collection, the orquideario municipal, and the municipal garden, where they grow plants for the city's landscaping. When I get there, it's almost siesta time for the orchids, and a gardener indicates that the place will close in a few minutes. I hustle through the shady displays of orchids, some just green tongues of leaves, some blooming, speckled and brilliant. Beyond the hedge and fence that holds the greenhouse and garden, I see a path I'd been planning to explore, but there's no exit to the path. I look at my map and realize I'd have to go to the opposite end of the zoo, to the entrance, and walk blocks and blocks to get back to this spot. While I'm pondering what to do, a group of teenagers climbs through a gap in the fence and hedge and enters the garden, heading toward the zoo. The path looks shady as it follows the Río Zamora. I slip over to the gap, look through. There's a drainage ditch and then a go-kart track bordering the path.

When I think no one is looking, I hop through the hedge, leap the ditch, and then hurry along the track until I reach the pebbled path, which leads north quietly along the river, past a salvage yard with a mountain of old refrigerators behind chain link and razor wire. Then it leaves behind its shade trees, skirts backyards and chickens and barking dogs, and passes through stretches of just grass and weeds and occasional tied-up cows. I'm not really in the city anymore. In addition to shoe treads and bike tracks and the hoofprints of cows, a trail of strange divots follows the path, and while I'm trying to imagine what animal or machine made this dotted line, I look up and see a little girl, hurrying along, holding the hand of a woman in stilettos.

Consider the conditions in which zoos exist. In 2002 in the West Bank, during the Second Intifada, Israeli gunfire spooked a giraffe, who hit his head and died of a stroke. His mate miscarried. The zoo's veterinarian, not wanting to waste the body of the male or the stillborn giraffe, stuffed them, and they're on display at the zoo. In December 2013, at the beleaguered Giza Zoo in Cairo, Egypt, a giraffe accidentally hanged herself from a wire and three bears died in what the zoo called a bear "riot"; tear gas wafted in from the nearby Nahda Square, where police were subduing demonstrators. In winter 2014, the Nashville Zoo discovered the bodies of nineteen enslaved African Americans while excavating for a new project. Also in the winter of 2014, a zoo in Copenhagen killed a healthy giraffe named Marius because he didn't have a good genetic makeup for their breeding program. They dismembered him in front of a public audience, including kids, and fed him to the lions. In August 2014, a zoo in Gaza was attacked in air strikes that killed a number of monkeys and a peacock, gazelle, lion, and fox. The remaining animals grew hungry and sick. A crew from CNN visited and brought the lions dead chickens. In September 2014, at a Bangkok crocodile farm and zoo, a depressed elderly woman threw herself into a pond with a thousand crocodiles, where she was devoured. The same month in New Delhi, a young man climbed over the railing into the white tiger enclosure and was mauled to death. Children watching threw sticks and stones at the tiger. In June 2015, flash flooding breeched the zoo in Georgia's capital Tbilisi, and animals escaped into the city, including lions, bears, and wolves. A news photo shows a man with a tranquilizer gun aiming at a confused hippo wading in flooded waters washing against a Swatch watch store.

The Sài Gòn Zoo and Botanical Garden is full of penguins—neat, sleek, white-bellied birds with their mouths agape. They stand every fifty feet or so along the paved paths, baked in the tropical heat, waiting for trash. I've seen these guys before, in the heart of a rocky island cave in Hạ Long Bay, along the coast of northern Việt Nam. The cave, which our guide called Amazing Cave, boasted an illuminated phallic rock formation at its heart. The cave, phallic rock or no, was truly amazing, but the anomalous penguin garbage cans were just odd. There aren't any real penguins at the Sài Gòn Zoo.

The Sài Gòn Zoo is actually full of storks, real storks, lesser adjutant storks to be exact. They're on display in a big glass enclosure with a concrete floor and small pond, but they're also just walking around all over the place—at another outdoor pond dolloped with giant lily pads around which people are picnicking, along the paths lined with penguins, next to a statue of a bear eating a banana by the snack shack. Their heads look wooden, reddish and mostly bald, with a few wispy feathers. Their beaks, torpedo pointed and too heavy to belong to the thin, orange necks, seem as though someone has attached a long costume beak onto each stork, with an invisible piece of elastic holding it in place. The storks meander down the zoo's asphalt paths with the human visitors and sit on branches over ponds sunning their wide, black wings. Do they know they're in a zoo?

The peacocks also ignore boundaries. There's one on top of another bird's cage. Another pecking around a garden hose between two enclosures. There's one taking a nap in the great hornbill's display, snuggled up next to a hornbill. In a cage designated for peacocks, a rat runs back and forth, eating the birds' food.

A slideshow at the top of the zoo's website depicts an array of animals one assumes one might encounter at the zoo, though this isn't a good assumption. There aren't, for instance, any red pandas. Nor are there any hummingbirds. There are, in fact, giraffes, though none of the pictured baobab trees. On the English version of the zoo's website, the animals are sorted into three categories: birds, reptiles, and "interesting." When I translate what's on the Vietnamese version of the website, the "interesting" animals are now classified as "exciting." The exciting animals are pretty much everything that isn't a bird or reptile. One of the exciting animals is *Ratufa bicolor*. The website also features a "Rules Tour" with a link leading to a page that says "Regulations," where nothing is listed.

Here is what you will also not find at the Sài Gòn Zoo: legions and legions of honking motorbikes. The zoo is a pause of green and relative quiet in the ever-moving, people- and building-packed city. Visitors stroll unhurried and buy snacks to feed themselves and animals. They take spins on amusement park rides, such as a swinging dragon affixed to a base decorated with a smiling bunny standing next to a carrot and a squirrel carrying a basket of nuts. Fragrant blossoms hang from branches where native birds hop and tweet and butterflies settle. Families pose in front of the elephants, who reach their trunks over electrified wires to slurp up carrots and long beans tossed by children. In the July heat, giant trees cast wide patches of shade.

I consider the often-touted conservation function of zoos, their role in protecting certain animals. In the years of war in Việt Nam, the Sài Gòn Zoo remained open to the public. Pictures taken of the zoo by American servicemen and workers during that time show a decorative pagoda on an island in a lily-dotted lake, families strolling down paths past elaborate plantings, women napping on the lawn with their conical hats pulled over their faces, smiling children. As the land that is now Cát Tiên National Park was being defoliated by American Agent Orange a hundred miles away, citizens of Sài Gòn could still hold chunks of sugarcane and have them snatched from their hands by an elephant's trunk.

Meanwhile, in 1973, in the north, the Hà Nội Zoological Park is said to have displayed the broken body of a US Air Force B-52 bomber that was brought down over its grounds, a popular exhibit situated next to a cage of mockingbirds.

I notice that zoos adore the word "ambassador." The Toledo Zoo website says that a pair of polar bear cubs "have an important future as ambassadors for a species." The same zoo's director eulogized a snow leopard that died in 2014 as "a tremendous ambassador for his species," and their curator for herpetology, upon acquiring a centenarian Galápagos tortoise, born in the wild, called the Galápagos tortoises "one of the most terrific ambassadors of any species." A cheetah cub rejected by his mother in spring 2014 is being raised at San Diego Zoo with a Rhodesian ridgeback puppy, according to the zoo's website, so they can be lifelong companions while the cheetah serves as a "cheetah ambassador." The puppy doesn't get to be an ambassador, perhaps because he has no wild cousins. Again and again on zoo websites and in zoo news, I find the word "ambassador," often in combination with "their wild cousins," as in "ambassador for their wild cousins." The word suggests that these animals have been sent by their nation of wild cousins on a mission to preserve their interests. As ambassadors, they should have the right to meet with the heads of state of the host sovereignty—the humans. I like to imagine how this would work were it true. I like to imagine that when engaged in diplomacy, the animal ambassadors might teach us something of patience and sacrifice. But I also like to imagine that some might consider using their highly evolved jaws.

Just beyond the entrance of the Smithsonian National Zoological Park in Washington, DC, a sign stuck beneath a few trees and among some decorations for the December ZooLights event explains that gray squirrels and black squirrels are the same kind of squirrel, just different colors. White squirrels are the same too. The sign also explains that the squirrels were once considered such pests that people in Ohio could pay their taxes with squirrel carcasses. By the late 1800s, squirrels were scarce, nearing extinction, and so in 1906 the zoo bought sixteen squirrels for a buck apiece and thus saved gray squirreldom. It's a good story, but I can't really find evidence of the brink anywhere else. The Ohio Department of Natural Resources says that the squirrel population rebounded when hunting laws were put into place by 1885. The ZooLights decorations near the squirrel sign are wire outlines of tulips and what looks like a monarch butterfly, covered in lights for the holiday season. The monarch butterfly population currently is in dangerous decline due in part to widespread use of herbicides that kill the caterpillar's only food—milkweed—and to illegal logging in their wintering grounds. But there's no sign here mentioning that tragedy in progress.

In addition to ZooLights, the zoo offers an opportunity to buy holiday gifts for the animals. The gifts include art supplies so the pandas can paint, balls with holes in them to provide stimulation for the collared peccaries and octopi, tractor tires for elephants to fling around, drainage tubes for ferrets to crawl in, PVC tubes for bears to do god-knows-what with, and iTunes gift cards so the apes can buy apps for their iPads.

My husband and I wander down the paved paths and happen upon a crowd leaning over the rails around a sunken enclosure, staring and pointing and exclaiming at what appears to be nothing. Then I see what they're pointing at—a fuzzy, rust-colored ball stuck in the branches of a bare tree. Red panda. It doesn't uncoil its neck from the ball to show us its face, doesn't do much of anything up there in the tree but be fuzzy and hint at its cuteness, which is enough for this crowd. I'm not sure if this red panda is Rusty, who escaped last summer and was later captured in the hip Adams Morgan neighborhood about a mile away.

We head toward exhibits that seem less crowded. The outdoor flight cage holds a number of birds—cormorants, peacocks, wood ducks, and mandarin ducks. The various ponds for the ducks must have powerful filtration systems, because I've raised ducks and know what ducks can do to water. The ducks fly about the cage. So do common songbirds, and I'm not sure if they're part of the exhibit or just birds that have slipped into the cage for free food.

We meander back to Asia Trail, where the elephants and giant pandas are on display. Another cute-craving crowd masses about the giant panda yard, where again nothing seems to be happening. Then, across the yard, about as far from the trail as possible, something moves. It's black and white and clearly a panda, but I get only a glimpse of its iconic World Wildlife Fund face before it turns away. There's a panda cub, Bao Bao, somewhere too, but she's not outside. Zoo panda fans can also watch the Panda Cam, which broadcasts the interior panda exhibit and shows, depending on when you tune in, pandas eating bamboo, pandas sleeping on manmade rocks up against a painted backdrop, or an empty panda habitat. In October 2013, the Smithsonian National Zoo closed because the United States government shut down when it couldn't agree on a budget. A photo of a sad kid in a bear-eared hat standing at locked zoo gates circled the internet. Panda Cam went offline.

The zoo is free to the public, supported by government funds. Budget cuts and limitations have stretched the zoo staff a bit thin, and several recent incidents suggest that the animals feel it, including the deaths of a kudu who ran into a wall and broke her neck, a red river hog who died of septicemia, and a gazelle who ran into a wall and died after being spooked by a zebra attacking a zoo staff member nearby. All of these incidents took place at the Cheetah Conservation Station, where, according to the zoo's website, visitors can "see a cheetah and zebras (separated by a fence) engaged in natural behaviors in a grassland setting similar to their natural savanna habitat." I wonder if part of natural behavior is sensing one's potential dinner/killer nearby and not being able to eat it/run away. On another part of the zoo's website, the popular cheetahs are described, predictably, as "ambassadors for their wild counterparts."

Though I do visit the octopi at the Invertebrate Exhibit, in the coming summer the Invertebrate Exhibit will close suddenly and for the foreseeable future, with no plans to reopen. Ninety-nine percent of species diversity on Earth will go unrepresented, without ambassadors, in the zoo. No one will be able to buy the octopi any gift balls.

Across from Panda Plaza lies Pachyderm Plaza, home of the Elephant Community Center, the names suggesting not a zoo but some sector of suburban America occupied by nonpeople. Then there are places where the line between nonpeople and people blurs, such as Prairie Dog Playland, where children can crawl through tunnels. The tunnels have holes for kids to pop up from to scan the playground for cutouts of prairie dog predators, like hawks and black-footed ferrets. There aren't, however, cutouts of ranchers with poison baits, fumigants, rifles, or traps.

We stop just past the elephants to use the Elephant Outpost, where a gift shop sells what a Smithsonian news release describes as "eco-friendly elephant products" and a snack shop provides refreshments that are "elephant friendly and do not contain palm oil." In the restroom, a sign over the toilet explains too many details about elephant excrement.

We follow the American Trail looking for some species that are more familiar, such as gray wolves, river otters, and beavers. At the beaver display, the lower parts of the trees are covered in wire mesh so the beavers can't do what beavers do, which is chomp on them. A male and a female zoo volunteer talk to the visitors and feed one of the beavers, Buzz, whose fur is wet and spiky. The male volunteer, who is bald, holds a plastic cup full of beaver treats, which he uses to reward Buzz for tricks, such as raising up his paws or opening his mouth. The volunteers clarify that these aren't really tricks but exercises that help the zoo staff when examining the beavers. We lean against the chain-link fence surrounding the exhibit, warm sun on our backs, waiting for Buzz to do another trick. Buzz grabs at the cargo pants of the male, who explains to the small crowd ready with cameras that the animals aren't forced to do the exercises; they aren't performers in a show. He says, "The animals here are all volunteers."

In a few months, Buzz will start showing his age—have trouble standing and walking—and the zoo will euthanize him. But right now, the human volunteer pulls a treat from his cup, and I know I should feel assured Buzz does exactly what he wishes.

in the classroom

The yellow and white checkered floor tiles—a predictable, cheerful pattern—lie. Nothing predictable or cheerful here. This walled compound of faded yellow three-story buildings once formed a school. Someone chose these tiles, thinking of young people. Or maybe there wasn't much thought put into the tiles. Maybe yellow and white checkered tiles are simply the typical school floor in Cambodia. The buildings, arranged around a courtyard, with balconies acting as hallways between the classrooms, resemble schools across Cambodia—a standard school architecture. Its former name, Tuol Svay Prey High School, comes from the area of the city where it is located. Another school in Phnom Penh has apparently taken the name. Looking at photographs of this newer school on its Facebook page, I see it has the same yellow and white tiles.

In 1976, when this school was no longer Tuol Svay Prey High School, it was transformed into S-21, a prison and interrogation center for the Khmer Rouge, where up to twenty thousand citizens were held and then executed. Only a dozen survived. In 1980, just months after the collapse of the Khmer Rouge regime, the compound opened as the Tuol Sleng Genocide Museum and has been operating as such since.

Rain hangs above, waiting in clouds, the afternoon I visit Tuol

Sleng. It's July and hot, and earlier in the day the sun shone bright. That morning, as my husband and I stood outside the walls of the Royal Palace on the stretch of Sothearos Boulevard closed to traffic, a child who couldn't have been more than two appeared in the middle of the empty six-lane road. I don't know where she came from. With hair cropped close, she wore only an oversized pink dress made for a much bigger child. She could've been a boy. I wasn't sure. The pink dress was my only clue. Her shadow moved along the pavement, longer than she was tall. She had bare feet and placed them carefully, one in front of the other, on the white lines marking the lanes, following the line past us and to the barriers that held back morning traffic. There was no one else around. No parents waiting on a nearby corner. No saffron-robed monks keeping a watchful eye. Across the boulevard, only an empty swath of green park and then some palm trees and the river leading to the Mekong. I wasn't sure what to do. The girl seemed to know where she was going, or at least know that she was following the white line. I spoke no Khmer and stood frozen, baffled. She reached the traffic barrier at the end of the block, turned left, rounded the corner, and disappeared behind the palace walls. I didn't try to track her.

In the small towns near where I live in northeast Ohio, schools are traditionally two- or three-story brick blocks—solid, with wood floors, chalkboards—built on theories of what makes us learn and keeps us healthy. Windows rise high to cast sun on desks, natural light that early twentieth-century designers felt should enter only over the left shoulders of seated students to keep them from straining their eyes. Straight hallways leading to stairs leading to outside for quick egress onto calm, green lawns. Symmetrical and stately.

Where is it? The old school at the heart of the town near my house is gone, its shadow now sunlight on grass. The grass belies what's missing, what was here, the landmark of the community, the doors the community passed through. I'd been taking it for granted, its brick and glass, its architecture of permanence on this corner. Now I can see past where it stood to the block of houses beyond, homes suddenly facing an expanse of nothing. They're knocking down places around here, school by school. Five, six, seven. The old schools are inconvenient and costly. Daily, I drive past a blond-brick elementary school. The crossing guard steps into traffic, waves her stop sign. Backpacks drooping, children pass by, steered by a sidewalk to the school's front doors. Built in 1928, the school has elegant arches framing the windows above its twin entrances. In a few months, nothing will stand here. Morning and afternoon traffic will speed along unimpeded.

My mail on February 27, 2013, consists of the usual coupons and catalogs. In the pile, I find a four-page newsprint ad for the local Great Lakes Outdoor Supply store. The first line of sale items includes a Smith and Wesson M&P 15 semiautomatic assault rifle, limit one per customer. Farther down the page, I see a fifty-round drum magazine for a Glock 9mm pistol going for $89.99. The tagline for GlockStore's YouTube demonstration of the magazine reads, "Now you can load up on Tuesday and shoot to Wednesday." There are lots of .22-caliber handguns and a bunch of styles of thirty-round magazines, limit twenty mags per customer. If you buy 260 rounds of ammo, you can get a free ammo box. There's something called a Micro-Uzi available for $14.99; it's a realistic-looking air gun and, according to the ad, "fun to shoot!" I weigh this all in my mind, the way the Carry-Lite Peep'n Tom Gobbler Decoy—which comes with a photorealistic tail fan, though you can use your own real, dried tail fan if you've got one—shares the page with the Glock drum mag.

One year ago to the day, on February 27, 2012, shortly after 7:30 in the morning, a seventeen-year-old (boy? young man?) entered a school in another small town eighteen miles from where I live. Classes hadn't started yet, and students were hanging out and eating breakfast in the cafeteria. The school sprawls, a collection of pale brick structures built between the 1950s and 1970s. News footage taken from a helicopter depicts the school's series of flat roofs speckled with snow. The teen didn't attend this school but would wait there every day for his bus to a nearby alternative school. Later in the morning, around 9 a.m., he was sitting on the side of a road telling a police officer that he'd shot some people. When asked why, he said, "I don't know." He'd opened fire in the cafeteria with a .22-caliber Ruger semiautomatic pistol and hit four students. Three died.

We arrive at Tuol Sleng by tuk-tuk, the carts pulled by motorbikes that serve as taxis in Phnom Penh. Our driver says he'll wait for us. He'd been hoping to take us on to another spot out of the city, the Choeung Ek killing fields. The two museums seem to be marketed by tuk-tuk drivers as a morbid package deal: first visit S-21, then see where many of the prisoners were taken to be executed. At one of the city's street markets, I noticed a parked motorbike advertising the tour. Painted on his gas tank were the words "Killing Fields Best Price." We don't have time to see Choeung Ek, though, because the killing fields close at 5 p.m.

Maybe because of the impending rain, there aren't many other people at the museum. A week earlier, outside Hà Nội, we spent an afternoon at a similarly constructed school building—though it was the bright yellow of new paint with spotless shining floors—at the campus of an organization called Vietnam Friendship Village, founded by an American veteran of the Vietnam War to help children with physical and developmental disabilities likely caused by the lingering effects of Agent Orange on the environment. We moved along the balcony connecting the second-floor classrooms, popping in to observe the kids, who either shied away from or begged for our attention. We crouched next to their desks and helped them draw circles or perform basic math—very basic math since I could only count to three in Vietnamese. The school also trained the students in skills like sewing gym shorts and crafting delicate artificial flowers so they could find work out in the world. A few years earlier a flood had inundated the buildings of the village, but there was no sign of the extensive damage left behind after the water receded.

The US Department of Health and Human Services Centers for Disease Control and Prevention put out a report on Youth Risk Behavior. The cover features a photo with the caption "Group of Adolescents Engaged in Recess and Study Time." In the picture, five clean and racially diverse teens—three boys, two girls—sit on a picnic table, smiling at the camera, notebooks stiff in hands, a glowing orange basketball at their feet. The image is clearly a stock photo, nothing realistic whatsoever about the students' composition or posture. They possess neither acne nor tattoos. The paper in their notebooks is blank. They aren't engaging in recess or study time. They're models, posed, some photographer's ideal teenagers. They smile and smile, an antidote to the contents of the report.

The report, created from a 2011 survey, tells me things that make me sad all along the continuum of ways to feel sad. During the thirty days prior to the survey, 32.8 percent of high school students had texted or emailed while driving, 38.7 percent had drunk alcohol, 23.1 percent had used marijuana, and 18.1 percent had smoked cigarettes. During the seven days prior to the survey, 5.7 percent had not eaten vegetables other than french fries or potato chips. During the twelve months prior to the survey, 7.8 percent had attempted suicide. Also during the thirty days prior to the survey, at some point in time, 16.6 percent had carried a weapon and 5.1 percent had carried a firearm. Over 5 percent had carried a weapon on school property.

Tuol Sleng's classrooms make me think of my own classrooms, as a student and as a teacher. A classroom creates an orderly place, chairs circling tables or paired with desks in rows. Students enter, they're accounted for and taught, and then they leave. At regular intervals, the process begins again—daily, yearly, and finally, generationally.

A few classrooms of the school/prison/museum display hundreds of photos taken of prisoners who arrived at S-21. The photographs of the prisoners of Tuol Sleng are deathly school pictures. The prisoners pose with numbers pinned to their shirts. One shirtless boy has a number pinned through the skin near his collarbone. Some have placards hanging from their necks. They're men and women and children, boys and girls. Some of the women hold infants. The girls have chin-length hair. The adults seem eerily composed. The photos form an enormous grid of faces, like a yearbook. The wood-framed stands displaying the photos look much like the portable chalkboard in my classroom, though where the slate would be, a population of the dead stares out from behind glass. The photographs are almost all taken face on, except for a few side shots that demonstrate the apparatus holding each prisoner's head and body in place, a brace invisible in the head-on shots. In addition to these photos of the prisoners when they were living, the exhibit contains some pictures of the prisoners after they were executed—throats slit. Some executions took place on the grounds of the school and many others miles away, at the Choeung Ek killing field.

Like the few other visitors gazing uncomfortably at the photos, I'm not sure what to do. I take pictures of the display, photos which show not only the victims but my own face reflected in the glass, obscured by the camera.

In 1979 the Vietnamese drove the Khmer Rouge from Phnom Penh and discovered the atrocities at S-21. In the classrooms, they found fourteen bodies shackled to metal bedframes, people executed before the Khmer Rouge fled. Today, in the classrooms where the bodies were found, the beds, shackles, and metal ammunition boxes used as toilets remain, as do black-and-white photos posted on the walls taken of the swollen and shiny cadavers. In one photo, two birds stand on a man's body. At first I think the birds are crows, but then I recognize their posture. They're chickens, bantam sized.

Back home, I stumble on a film made by a crew entering S-21 when the bodies were discovered. In it, a dead man lies stretched on a fiber mat atop a metal bed, ankles shackled. Next to him, a chicken scratches in that particular chicken way—automatic and absentminded. At first, I think this is a film of the same man in the photograph, but when I compare the two images, I see they are different men, different chickens. The classroom's windows have no panes, only wooden shutters that open and close. On sidewalks all over Phnom Penh, chickens cluck and peck. Of course chickens could just wander in. But still, this juxtaposition of the horrible with the homely, ordinary creatures of routine perplexes me.

In 1979, when S-21 was discovered, I was in the second grade. My school was a mishmash of old and new. The original building had been constructed in 1913, but my classes were held in a new addition designed according to the "open concept" theory popular in the 1970s. It was a space the size of three regular classrooms shared by three teachers and two grades, and students could move between grade levels, depending on their skills in each subject. I took a class with the third graders that studied things like ancient civilizations, and I remember stories of human sacrifice and images of Tikal's mysterious pyramids, which remind me vaguely of the ruins of Angkor Wat in Cambodia.

In 1979, when S-21 was discovered and I was in the second grade, the United States supported the Chinese-backed Khmer

Rouge remnants exiled to the countryside, fearful of the Vietnam-ese who had dislodged the Khmer Rouge from power. In the years leading up to the overthrow of the Khmer Rouge, the United States and United Nations had little to say about the events in Cambo-dia. According to a study about news coverage of the genocide, between 1975 and 1978, the three major US news networks spent almost no time on Cambodia. CBS featured the most reporting on the subject, which clocked in at a total of twenty-eight minutes and fifty-five seconds from April 1975 to December 1978. In 1979 the Khmer Rouge was still recognized as the holder of Cambodia's seat in the United Nations. It retained the seat, alone and then with a coalition of other resistance forces, until 1990.

The more than 1,500 guards and interrogators at S-21 were young people, many between fifteen and nineteen years old. At ages as young as ten, they were indoctrinated into the Khmer Rouge from rural, peasant families and given brutal training in which they were told to forget their parents and embrace instead the orga-nization. They were chosen because they were blank slates, with few life experiences or expectations or memories. When I look at pictures of young men working at S-21, I recognize the soft, unfinished features of boyhood. A 1996 UN report titled "Impact of Armed Conflict on Children" states, "The lure of ideology is particularly strong in early adolescence, when young people are developing personal identities and searching for a sense of social meaning."

What happened to the students the guards displaced, the stu-dents who had attended Tuol Svay High School? Surely, those stu-dents were evacuated from the city for hard labor in rural work groups, where many must have died from starvation or execution, their lives swapped with those of the young guards, who suddenly found themselves in a school, not as students but as intimidators, torturers, and murderers—or maybe as students of intimidation, torture, and murder.

The Khmer Rouge leaders who recruited the young people and oversaw their "reeducation" have yet, for the most part, to be brought to justice in a court. Debate over whether there should be trials and of what kind lingered for decades. Cambodia's prime minister, Hun Sen, a former Khmer Rouge himself, once said in response to the plan for trials, "We should dig a hole and bury the past and look ahead to the twenty-first century with a clean slate." In 2006 a UN-backed tribunal in Cambodia was formed to investigate and try the leaders for crimes against humanity and war crimes. The tribunal, called the Extraordinary Chambers in the Courts of Cambodia, or the Khmer Rouge Tribunal, has cost $330 million. Only three people have been convicted. The first was the man known as Duch, who became the warden of S-21. Two others—Nuon Chea and Khieu Samphan—were leaders in the regime. Pol Pot, the number one leader, died years earlier. Ieng Sary died in March 2013, before a verdict was reached in his case. Ieng Sary's wife, Ieng Thirith, was deemed unfit for trial because of dementia.

An illusion, the safety of schools. We've learned that again and again. I was a young high school teacher in Oregon when the shootings at Columbine in Colorado occurred. A year later in

Oregon, a boy killed his parents, walked into his high school, and shot off fifty rounds, killing two people. Schools began to talk of lockdowns, of places to hide. I evaluated my classroom for vulnerability, and sometimes, reluctantly, I evaluated my students. But it's easier to assess a building than it is a troubled mind that might belong to the 5.4 percent carrying a weapon to school. From the school grounds, I could peer in the wall-to-wall windows of my classroom and know exactly what was inside, see what anyone else peering in would see.

Outside S-21 ran the streets of Phnom Penh, a ghost city, population removed. Now outside Tuol Sleng: a beauty parlor, a shop selling shoes and handbags, a second-floor apartment for rent, its balcony decorated in potted palms, staring across into the windows of the museum's classrooms.

While some of the classrooms contain the displayed photos, others remain as they were, holding rooms and cells for prisoners. In some rooms, numbers line the walls where prisoners lay on the floor, shackled. In others, the rooms are divided into brick or concrete-block or wooden cells about the size of a bathtub, three to four floor tiles wide, each with a numbered wooden door. I stick my head into a cell—the odor ammoniac, warm and infirm. I envision the faces from the photos in the cells, and as soon as I do, I wish I hadn't. Each corridor of cells ends with a door punched through the concrete wall of the classroom, leading to the next classroom with its corridor of cells, leading to next, and so on. In the last classroom, in place of a door cut into the wall, the green expanse of a chalkboard bears faded writing in Khmer. Even in the rooms that now hold displays, I notice at intervals the yellow and white tiles missing where the walls of cells once stood, now removed. Loops for shackles protrude from the floor.

In the 2003 documentary *S-21: The Khmer Rouge Killing Machine,* a former guard reenacts his surveillance of prisoners shackled on the floors of the holding rooms. In an empty classroom, he paces between two imaginary lines of bodies, shouting for half of them to stand. He frisks emptiness for contraband, for pens they could use to slit their wrists or screws they could swallow to kill themselves. He demands order. He yells at them to sit. Then he turns and does the same to the other half. He seems entranced by this memory, conjuring up the prisoners from nothing, pointing his finger at imaginary infractions, asserting his long-gone authority.

My classroom feels tolerant and supportive most days, but when I sense I've been disrespected—or, more accurately, the process of learning has been disrespected—I don't hesitate with my rebuke. Sometimes outside of my classroom and school I struggle to turn off the teacher inside me, the person impatient with churlishness or whining or pushing the rules. I've often found myself raising my eyebrow and giving the long stare to some kid in a store or restaurant. "You wouldn't get away with that," I think, "in my classroom."

The young comrades of S-21 clearly feared for their lives. They, too, were tortured for minor infractions and imaginary offenses, just as the prisoners they guarded and interrogated were. As time passed, the Khmer Rouge began to prey on itself. A third of the guards at S-21 fell victim to S-21.

The museum offers few signs to help visitors navigate the experience. In the first classroom building, Building A, a sign shows the face of a man with an exaggerated toothy smile inside a red circle with an X. I understand the universal symbol for "don't," but don't *what?* Don't smile? Don't joke around? Don't be happy? On a wall covered in graffiti, another red circle contains a hand holding a pen. The English-language graffiti on the museum walls reflects mostly sentiments like, "Don't let this shit happen ever again! Please!" or "Tragic" or "Replace hate" or simply "R.I.P." But I also read, "Killian Waterford 2010 boss sex tourist!!"

The starkness of the museum is meant, I assume, to speak for itself. The museum was created by the Vietnamese, designed by the same man who created the War Remnants Museum, formerly known as the Exhibition House for Crimes of War and Aggression, in Hồ Chí Minh City, which I visit the next week. In that museum, numerous signs explain everything from the Chinook helicopter, tanks, and other captured armaments decorating the museum courtyard to the American antiwar movement. While we're there, busloads of school kids around ten years old pour into the museum, uniformed and clamorous. "Whatsyourname?" they shout at me again and again. I try to answer, but they move on, laughing. For a while, they sit quietly on the floor of the lobby for a lecture, but then they're released into the museum halls, where I encounter them at the Agent Orange exhibit. Color photos of children with severe birth defects line the walls, with explanations about their homes and care. The students point and gawk, some giggling. They crouch, transfixed, around a glass case holding several deformed fetuses drifting in yellowish liquid. There are no teachers around.

The UN report offers a clear recommendation for helping children caught in conflicts—school. Education "gives shape and structure to children's lives and can instill community values, promote justice and respect for human rights and enhance peace, stability and interdependence." The report also acknowledges that schools and teachers are often targets of attacks.

I'm a teacher. My husband is a teacher. If we'd taught at S-21 when it was Tuol Svay Prey High School, we would be dead, because the Khmer Rouge executed the educated and the educators. Only 10 percent of the secondary school teachers in Cambodia, around two hundred people, survived the Khmer Rouge regime. The education system of the country was virtually erased. Though many teachers fell victim to the regime, a few also led it. Pol Pot had been a schoolteacher. Ieng Thirith had been a schoolteacher. Duch, the warden at S-21, was a former schoolteacher, as was his superior, deputy prime minister Son Sen.

As I slip from corrupted classroom to corrupted classroom, studying the tragedy of S-21, my thoughts repeat, "This is a school. This could be any school. This could be my school." I picture my own classroom, students, and even the benign order of my lessons transformed into something deeply dangerous. It might not be genocide—there are many shades of cruelty, injustice.

My initial reaction to this place is, "How could this happen?" But this seems like a question asked too late. Perhaps the real question is, "Why do we let this happen?" Or "Do I let this happen?" Or "Will I let this happen?"

Columbine High School destroyed the library where ten of the victims were murdered, replacing it with an atrium. The Virginia Tech building where a gunman killed thirty-two people got a million-dollar makeover. The Amish school where five students were killed in 2006 was knocked down within ten days of the shooting. Sandy Hook Elementary, where twenty-six children and adults were killed in 2012, was demolished and rebuilt on the same site. Sometimes a place of horror demands a monument, and sometimes it demands erasure. How do we know which is which? Many Cambodians have felt conflicted about the Genocide Museum, either because they would like to move on or because they feel it stands in for true justice, for the trials of Khmer Rouge officials who orchestrated the horror. There are even some who believe that S-21 is simply Vietnamese propaganda, a story invented to justify their invasion of Cambodia, which is what the Khmer Rouge claimed in the aftermath of its discovery. Maybe a place demands a monument when we're still trying to unravel its significance. Maybe a place demands erasure when we resist figuring out what it means. Maybe we don't move on; we just give up on trying to decipher what we can't understand.

A misty rain starts to fall as we head to the exit of the museum to search for our tuk-tuk driver. I notice a white-haired man in a collared short-sleeved shirt sitting at a table with some books and magazines. I stop, curious, thinking this is a strange place for souvenirs. It turns out he's a former mechanic named Chum Manh, also known as Chum Mey, one of the seven prisoners who survived S-21 who have come forward since 1979, and one of only four known to be still living. The entire museum feels haunted, and this man could be a ghost, but though his presence is uncanny and incomprehensible, lingering within the place of his imprisonment, he is very much alive, a human being in the present tense. For ten US dollars, he's selling copies of a magazine called *Searching for the Truth* produced by the Documentation Center of Cambodia. The issue is from 2001, and it features his story. I buy one, and he signs it. He's a tidy man with blue-gray eyes. A woman assisting him slides the magazine into a plastic bag emblazoned with hearts and the slogan "That's wonderful!" We're ready to leave when she stops us and suggests that we get our picture taken with him. I balk, feeling perhaps this makes him a souvenir. But she's insistent, and I don't want to be rude, so I hand her my camera. My husband and I sit down on either side of Chum Manh in plastic chairs that appear to be placed for this purpose. I can't imagine what Chum Manh is thinking. In the photo, my husband and I stare at the camera, resigned to our roles. Chum Manh is composed—he's done this before. Across his chest, he holds the signed magazine with his picture on the cover, identifying himself for the viewer. In front of us, a banner hangs from the table, explaining what seems impossible: "Former victim at S-21."

patas

LOJA, ECUADOR

The chickens hang in a row, a hook through each left leg, some legs with scaly yellow feet still attached, some ending at the drumstick. Some of the attached feet are only semiattached, cut through the joint so that they dangle, fatty soles waving. Some chickens, split open along the belly, expose the ovaries' bright sacs of yolks, the nascent eggs inside the birds waiting for whites and shells. Others remain mostly whole, bumpy skin buttery—fatty tails over cave-like holes leading to hollow bellies. Beneath these curtains of chickens, white-tile counters covered in steel trays with more chickens and parts of chickens. Behind the chickens, women in aprons selling chickens, their booths festooned with fuzzy green garland, lingering from Christmas. One woman points to the orange cluster of yolks, tells me, "Pollo bonito. Con huevos." I understand this. I can say "pollo." But I can't say much else. The words, las palabras, nestled and slippery in my brain.

I'm at the Mercado San Sebastián, near downtown, and I'd like to ask if I can buy some feet, only the feet, to make some stock. Los pies. I know this means feet, but is it the same word for chickens as it is for humans? I don't know, so I, well, chicken out. I've been in Ecuador for five weeks and in Loja for a few days. When I mentioned to Ecuadorians elsewhere that I would be staying in Loja for a month, they'd tell me the Spanish that people speak here is "lengua muy pura," very pure language, whatever that means. My Spanish is anything but pure, a garbled residue from classes I took over twenty years ago.

Later, I sit in my one-room apartment, staring at my propane cook-top, planning to head to my local market, where I'll ask for feet. I practice saying, "Es posible que comprar solo unos pies?" which is probably not the correct way to ask if I can buy feet. I think the "que" is just something I've thrown in there, because I have a habit of throwing "que" into sentences, especially questions. The "pies" seems wrong too. And then, after I ask my question, what? Another word I throw into conversations a lot is "quizás." Perhaps. Perhaps she'll understand me. And perhaps, when she answers me, I'll understand her.

The next day, I head up the park path near my apartment to my neighborhood market. The path runs along Río Malacatos and past a small sports court where some weekday mornings a young man in a track suit leads dozens of local women and men in bai-loterapia, a bouncy, chest-thrusting, hip-torturing, dance-based exercise class funded by the government of Ecuador to get citizens in shape. I attended once, but I've been too embarrassed by my rhythm to return. The park path also passes by many loose dogs, who nap in the grass or trail alongside me as I walk. I hesitate to call them strays, because most seem to have homes they return to, where I notice them in the evening waiting outside the gates for their owners to let them in.

On Saturday mornings, the stretch of street along the park path fills with the feria libre, a farmers' market where people from the countryside come to Loja to sell their goods. On tarps on the street lie piles of plantains and green bananas, knowns as guineos, used for making Loja's signature soup, repe lojano. Old women hunker on overturned five-gallon buckets and shuck peas or corn. Cooks grill cuy—guinea pigs—and sell them hot and mahogany-skinned. Boys stand behind enormous bags of limóns, the tiny green limes I can't resist, hawking them for one or two cents apiece. I tend to buy at least fifty, then try to figure out what I should do with them. Women dip fresh milk from cans into plastic bags. Card tables flash with fresh greens, bowls of potatoes, fat carrots, tomate de árbol (tree tomatoes), pineapples, yuca roots, and guaba pods—a fruit that looks like a giant green bean with inedible dark seeds cradled in an edible, sweet, cottony fuzz. All along, the vendors cry out their prices: "Un dólar, un dólar, un dólar!" or "Veinticinco, veinticinco!" which sounds, in their sales chant, like "Baintsing!"

As it turns out, my market, Mercado la Tebaida, is a tiny building compared to San Sebastián and its row of chicken vendors. I'd imagined a lot of feet here to choose from, but my market has only one chicken vendor today, tucked in a corner to the side of about a dozen booths selling produce. She, too, has some Christmas garland, but only a few chickens, and on her tray, a small pile of organs and feet. Another woman is placing an order, so I loom off to the side, waiting to recite my question. In order to look like a serious shopper, I've bought from one of the produce booths a bunch of chard for twenty-five cents, which dangles in a bag from my wrist. While my language comprehension is weak, I'm a fair guesser, so when the chicken vendor glances at me and asks me a question, I'm pretty sure she wants to know what the heck I'm doing, looming, staring at her few yellow feet, which don't look quite as tidy as some of the feet I saw yesterday—skin peeling off, nails intact, brown calluses on the soles, blood at the bare joints. But they don't look that bad either, so I ask my question, pointing toward the feet.

A pause. Both women frown at me. "Para sopa," I explain. Or try to. Then the customer says, "Ah . . ." and some word I can't catch. The vendor nods, grabs a few feet and a handful of organs. Though I love chicken liver, I haven't added it into my equation. So I say again, "Solo pies." "Pies" is clearly the wrong word, but she puts down the organs and grabs a few more feet. The other customer smiles, with what I'd like to think is approval, and says, "Caldo muy rico." I use my third overused phrase, "Me gusta," because soup is indeed pleasing to me, as many things are.

"Ochenta," the vendor says, packing the feet into a palm-sized transparent bag. I dig eighty cents out of my wallet. She says something else, gesturing at a stack of black plastic bags with handles. I hear "negra" and guess that she's asking me if I want another bag, which I do, because I feel a little odd strolling down the park path carrying a visible bunch of feet.

I think the word the customer used might have been "patas," which does, in fact, mean animal feet or paws, but I could swear it had an "-ita," the diminutive, at the end, as in "little feet." When I look up "patitas de pollo," however, it seems often to mean chicken fingers or nuggets, as in breaded hunks of ambiguous chicken meat meant for people under five years old, though sometimes it does seem also to mean very un-ambiguous feet.

In my apartment, I wash my patas and cut off their toenail joints, pressing hard with the knife until they snap, nails clinking into the stainless steel sink, a nightmare pedicure. I add each of the eight feet to my pot with some water and onions and garlic and light my propane cooktop stove. My apartment has two windows—

one near the sink—which look out onto the courtyard shared by my neighbors: my landlady, her daughter, her sister and nephew, an American couple, and a renter who lives above me, of whom I've seen only two glimpses in the days I've been here, a man I think of as "the professor" because that's what I believe he is. The windows do little to keep sound in or out, so I hear pretty much everyone's business if it takes place in the courtyard. That is to say, I hear their business but understand only what I can translate. It's a gray afternoon, a little cool in the low sixties, and, circling the neighborhood, the garbage truck plays its own particular musical tune to let folks know it's picking up garbage; the melody sounds a bit like the beginning of a sonata. In the background, the crowing of roosters, confused by the dark skies.

The feet are my doorway. The next week, I head to Mercado Centro, the big market downtown. This market has vendors selling vegetables on both the far north and the far south ends, with stands selling beef and pork and fish in the middle. The two ends have different personalities. The south is poorly lit with the mostly female vendors yelling "Qué busca?" at me as I pass by their stalls. They don't seem to smile. The aisles are busy with people, with children and the occasional dog knocking into my knees. On the north end, the lights are brighter, and the vendors all wear cheerful red aprons. They may ask what I'm looking for, but gently. And they smile. After I buy a bag of shelled peas, one vendor points at my hand and says what I hear as "plata." I look at my silver wedding ring. "No," she says, pointing still. I frown. She mimics someone pulling a small zipper. She's concerned that my wallet, which closes with a zipper, is still open. She smiles maternally. I'm a niña, tonta enough to walk around with a wallet full of coins and the zipper undone. And I probably am.

Another vendor gets excited when I tell her I'm looking for a particular kind of hot pepper, small and red with black seeds inside. I've seen them only once at a street market. She raises her eyebrows when I explain, "Ají rojo con negro en el centro." I don't know the word for seeds, but she understands, because she digs a few out from behind her piles of chard and potatoes and tomatoes and onions, as though from a secret cache, nodding. Despite this special attention, this soft sell, the north end doesn't seem to have nearly as many customers.

I see that there are three chicken vendors in one corner of the north side vegetable stands, each with their chickens hanging up, their trays of parts. I see a few feet in a tray and ask the lady for "patas para caldo, una libra y media." She has tidy feet, whacked off below the joint, sliced through at various points, making them easier to pull apart, like a perforated line in a notebook. She piles them into a sack, weighs them on her scale until there's a pound and a half. It seems like a lot more feet, in part because it's just the feet, not the whole lower leg section. She slides the sack into a black plastic bag.

This time, I've bought a pair of scissors at a paper shop for seventy-five cents. Instead of whacking off the toenails, I snip them with the scissors, sometimes extracting a thin white tendon that looks like dental floss. I peel off any loose skin, trim the brown calluses on the pads of the feet. The feet float around the broth, simmering for hours and hours as I add more water now and then. The windows steam up. Late at night, I put the broth in my little refrigerator, and the next day, it's a solid mass of protein with circles of fat on top, which I scoop off with the spoon.

The next afternoon, I reheat the broth and strain it. The cooked feet have fallen apart into joints and skin and soft flesh, but the flavor is mostly boiled out. I gnaw on a few watery toes, toss the rest. To my broth I add fresh shelled green peas and beans, chard, and the little pink-and-white roots known in Ecuador as mellocos. My landlady's daughter makes fun of me because at first I thought mellocos were potatoes, and I told her I put them in soup. She says they are traditionally cooked then served cold, with lime, as a salad. My soups are a mishmash of ingredients, because everything looks so good at the markets I want to throw it all in, even if the vegetables don't make sense together. During my stay in Loja, when it's too rainy to wander, I make variations of feet soup—with corn, with beans, with yuca, with cilantro and hot red pepper and lime and tomato salsa. With mellocos.

I've been wondering about those yolks inside the chickens, developing globes in different sizes. Would you cook them separately or inside the bird? Weeks later, on my last day in Ecuador, at the Mercado Santa Clara in Quito, as I eat lunch at the counter of a small stand, I find them in front of me. In a glass baking dish, piled on top of a whole roasted chicken, sit several golden-skinned backs, each with a clutch of cooked yolks, like yellow stones. I scan the posted menu, trying to figure out what their name might be. I'm curious and would like to try them, whatever they're called. But I already have an enormous plate of rice, potatoes, diced tomatoes, sauce, and a slab of lengua—thick, but tender, tongue.

paradise, earth

It's hot, the afternoon's humid air warmer than the temperature of the human body, and my husband and I have been in Việt Nam for only a few hours. On a street in Hà Nội's Old Quarter, we wander into a restaurant with a shady back courtyard garden and koi pond. In the pond, a small turtle pokes his head out of the water, oblivious to the terrapin on the menu. The waitress turns on a large oscillating fan affixed to the wall over our table, and we order two sixteen-ounce bottles of beer. The bottles weep in the heat, and the fan dries my sweat-soaked T-shirt. The beer is weak, but fragrant and cold. We're more curious than hungry. Cris ate breakfast on two flights this morning, and in Hà Nội we've already tried some bánh mì sandwiches—baguettes that were filled with cool pâté but were shorter on daikon radish, carrot, cucumber, and hot pepper than we'd hoped. Now we split an order of fried spring rolls and a dish of beef in claypot with crispy rice noodles. The restaurant is deserted. In the middle of the day in Old Quarter, things are quiet, and then business starts up again in the evening. A teenage girl brings our check, shyly testing her schoolbook English. We stumble out into the sun and around the corner to our hotel for a dose of air conditioning.

Before our trip, we bought many guidebooks about Việt Nam—each detailing its own take on food, language, customs, history—

which Cris read more thoroughly than I did because either I was unable to picture the things described or I distrusted what I did picture. One of the guidebooks tells us about the fourth emperor of the Nguyễn dynasty in Việt Nam, Tự Đức. Briefly the text mentions fifty-course meals cooked by fifty chefs, menus that never repeated a dish. Tự Đức was a scholar and poet but not the most effective ruler at a time when Việt Nam needed one, when France had gained control of the Mekong Delta and was vying for more.

In Việt Nam, whole stretches of streets form markets, and I could walk them for days. There's a purposelessness to looking at food you can't take home and cook that renders it all scenery and landscape. The market glows with fruits and vegetables spread out on flat, round baskets. Some I recognize from my time lingering in produce aisles of Asian markets back home—the long-stemmed water spinach; piled branches of purplish basil; gnarled ginger and galangal; bright green straws of garlic chives; shiny hearts of betel leaves; fragile, translucent star fruit; and prickly durian, bigger than footballs. Some are new to me—a vivid pink fruit shaped like a large egg and a long, white, rootlike vegetable with feathery leaves similar to mimosa. The pink fruit was on the fruit plate in our hotel room when we arrived, along with a banana, an Asian pear, and a cluster of lychees. We aren't sure what to do with the pink thing, which has a supernatural color, like a gerbera daisy. We leave it alone until we can conduct a little research. But the next day, it's been replaced with a red apple.

Tự Đức wasn't much loved by his people and had some trouble

holding onto his throne, in part because of questions of legitimacy. After his father, Emperor Thiệu Trị, died, the Vietnamese court chose youngest son Tự Đức over his older brother, Hồng Bảo, for emperor. Hồng Bảo made a grab for the throne in a coup, but the attempt was thwarted. One source says that in response, Tự Đức was forced to execute his brother and then, later, most of his brother's family. Another source says he sentenced Hồng Bảo to death by "live dissection," but their mother stepped in and asked that the sentence be commuted to life in prison, which didn't suit Hồng Bảo, so he hanged himself with a bedsheet.

In an attempt to try to get back the land lost in the Mekong Delta, Tự Đức chose a mandarin named Phan Thanh Giản to travel to France on a diplomatic delegation. In France, Phan Thanh Giản was awestruck by French technology—the roads, the gas lamps, the trains making the world small. His discoveries seemed to deflate his hopes. According to one source, when the emperor subsequently named him viceroy of the southern provinces, he basically handed the territory over to France—who had bigger ships, better guns, and well-armed soldiers—rather than fight for the region, declaring in a note to his troops, "The empire of our king is antiquated." Then he wrote a report to the emperor, returned all of his distinguished awards, and fasted for fifteen days, after which he took poison and died. According to another source, the territories were taken from him by the French while he was away negotiating an accord, and, too weak for the strong French, he reluctantly gave in to their demands. Then he fasted for seventeen days, and when that didn't kill him, took a fatal vinegar and opium combination, the tragic story ending with him stripped posthumously of his rank and awards by the emperor.

Tự Đức was upset by this loss to France as well. One source

quotes what it calls a public confession by the emperor: "Alone, I am speechless. My pulse is feeble, my body pale and thin, my beard and hair white. Though not yet forty, I have already reached old age, so that I lack the strength to pay homage to my ancestors every morning and evening. . . . Alas! the centuries are fraught with pain, and man is burdened by fear and woe. Thus we express our feelings, that they may be known to the world." When he wrote this, he was the same age I am now, on this trip to his country, and completing construction of his mausoleum on the Perfume River outside the Imperial City of Huế.

I'm sitting in my yard in Ohio reading about Tự Đức when my dog goes wild, sounding her fierce bark for strangers who've wandered into her space, the fur on her back standing up. I see a blue sedan in the driveway behind our house and trot over to apologize for the dog, thinking someone's here to read the meter. Then I notice through the open window the necktie, the smile, the telltale pamphlet in his hand. "No problem," the clean-cut man says, "I'm just dropping off some encouraging literature." As I hold the dog by her collar, he carefully backs out toward the road.

The *Watchtower* tract explains that the dead "cannot harm—or help—the living." It also tells me that "Jesus promised that 'those in the memorial tombs will . . . come out.' (John 5:28, 29) In harmony with God's original purpose, those resurrected as humans will have the opportunity to live on a paradise earth."

In the evening, at a well-lit restaurant with yellow walls and white tablecloths, we wipe our hands with cold, moist towels and dine on banana-flower salad, fried soft-shell crab with lime and pepper dipping sauce, shrimp paste on sugarcane, and water morning glory with garlic. We pay more than we should for a bottle of Australian chardonnay. We spy on the other tables as their food arrives, wondering what it is. We go back to our room and drink more wine, listening to motorbike horns as we fall asleep in a giant bed with down pillows.

In the morning, we head out early in search of breakfast—phở, the beef noodle soup Hà Nội is famous for. Even at six o'clock, large kettles simmer on sidewalks, surrounded by colanders of mung bean sprouts and greens, bowls of chopped and sliced raw meat or noodles or dried fish. Customers sit on short plastic stools at, or not at, the occasional short table outfitted with chili sauce, quartered limes, and the ubiquitous, singularly delicious fermented fish sauce, nước mắm. Women crouch in the midst of these elements and serve up steaming concoctions. Some of the stands have signs, some don't. We're new at this and a little hesitant. There aren't any other tourists out yet. Many local people we've met in Hà Nội have been extremely friendly, but in general the women who run these stalls look unapproachable—not necessarily angry but perhaps bitterly tired. Their seats are full, and they don't need us slowing things down.

We're searching for a restaurant we read about in our guidebook that supposedly has the best phở in Hà Nội. When we find it, it's not yet open, so we linger around, stopping into a café so Cris can have coffee with sweetened condensed milk. On the sidewalk outside the café, a group of men sit in small plastic chairs sipping coffee and smoking cigarettes. All morning long, we see cafés, each with men sitting drinking coffee, leisurely reading the paper, laughing and joking, and I begin to think the women crouching before their food stalls would have good reason to be grouchy.

We return to the phở shop, but it's still closed, probably forever. We notice down the street a sign that says "Phở Xào Phú Mỹ," and at the entrance, which is open to the sidewalk, a man stands over a kettle of broth on a burner. Next to him sits a basket of cooked noodles and bowls of raw beef. He speaks no English. We take a table in the back of the shop. The menu is posted on the wall, and each dish seems to be called phở something, so I thumb through our phrasebook, hoping to translate. At the phở shop we frequent back home, there are a dozen kinds of phở, with different combinations of beef and beef parts. It's already quite hot, and the fans above the tables blow good smells around the narrow space, a hint of star anise and ginger. Two men at another table are drinking tea and enjoying bowls of fragrant phở. A boy of about eight comes over to us and points assuredly at the menu, seeming confident he knows what we want. Okay, we say, nodding. A few minutes later, an old woman brings out two plates of noodles piled with beef and water spinach in a thick sauce, accompanied by a table salad of basil and lettuce and cucumbers. Not soup. We're not sure what to do, so we begin to dig in, mourning our light, tasty phở. Soon though, Cris proposes that we point to the soup everyone else is slurping and order two bowls. It's only about three dollars wasted on the misunderstanding, which to us seems like nothing. So we call the boy over, and the salty hot soup serves as paradoxical antidote to the rising heat of the day. As other patrons get up to go, I notice that many leave their soup unfinished, the broth remaining in the bowl, their glasses of tea nearly full, a testament to a kind of plenty by people who have suffered much scarcity. Later, when

I try to translate the shop's name, I can only come up with "noodle fried rich elegance" or else "noodle fried rich American."

The Vietnamese markets we visit look temporary, with low-hanging roofs constructed of tarps tied together. Cris has to bend over to walk through them. Vendors sit with their array of produce or meat in baskets and tubs, sometimes stacked on the Styrofoam coolers or crates they've used to transport the goods. At some carts, women cook tiny crabs or stuffed tofu or beef rolled in betel leaves, but most stalls feature raw ingredients, fresh and often alive. Fish swim in shallow plastic tubs. Ducks with their wings strapped to their bodies lie on the sidewalk. Chickens cluck in cages. Little mud crabs crawl over one another, trying to climb the slippery sides of their bowl. Soft-shell turtles crane their blueish necks, seeming vulnerable among the hard knots of snails in baskets, the grasping prawns in pots of water. At one market, a boy squats over a duck carcass, clutching the limp neck, scraping away the white feathers around its eye with a knife. I pass by a table and am startled by a faint explosion on the edge of my vision—frogs in a basket leaping against the net that holds them in.

Tự Đức's mausoleum was expansive and elaborate, and once it was built, he spent much of his time there in the palaces and temples or at the pavilion by the lake full of lotuses where he liked to write poetry. There's an island where he hunted, which is said to have been stocked with miniature deer. Stone elephants, horses, and mandarins watch over Tự Đức's mausoleum and the stone stele on which is written his eulogy. Empress Lệ Thiên Anh has her own tomb. Though she was his primary wife, he had over a hundred other wives and concubines, who also lived on the grounds of the mausoleum. The buildings have tile roofs and are decorated with mosaics made from broken porcelain dishes, smooth, curved bits with blue and light-jade glazes, some showing the ridged ring around the bottom of a bowl or plate. When I see these mosaics at the mausoleum and at the Imperial City of Huế, I wonder if anyone ever ate from the dishes, and if so, what meals they enjoyed.

For lunch, we hunker over plates of nem rán, fried pork spring rolls with mushroom and crab, and bowls of bún chả, grilled pork dipped in dark broth and eaten with noodles and fresh greens, herbs, and sprouts. We drink large bottles of beer, watch the women tending the blazing brazier or spooning hot liquid into plastic bags for orders to go. At night, we dine on mango salad with beef; bright pumpkin vines and garlic; squid, scallops, and shrimp cooked in a claypot; broth with field crab and fresh greens; and homemade ice cream. Our bottle of wine seems bottomless, the waitress in a red áo dài filling and refilling, waiting a few feet away, watching us sip. On the nighttime streets of Old Quarter, we weave through clusters of people perched on stools, drinking tea and beer, eating bowls of noodles and meat, chicken on rice, long baguettes, or dishes with nothing in them I can name.

In one source I read, Tự Đức is described as a "good man" and "devoted son" with "compassion for his people" and also as "a victim of Confucian tradition" and an "outstanding scholar." In another, he's a "romantic poet" and "weak ruler" who escaped from the world to his garden-like mausoleum. In another, he's described as "myopic," in another as having had a "sad life." Yet another describes him as "pusillanimous" and "sickly." He's sometimes an "ardent poet" and sometimes "ineffectual." Physically, he was small. A placard at his tomb describes him as "a frail aesthete," plagued with melancholy and superstition. It says: "A weak-willed man, he embroiled his land in numerous crises. Public morale sank ever lower, for he proved helpless in the face of natural disasters, famine, exploitive mandarins or powerful landowners. His arbitrary concessions and lack of political judgment abetted the French annexation of Vietnam, begun in the reign of Thiệu Trị, his father. By the time Tự Đức died, the entire country was under the yoke of colonial rule."

The mausoleum itself is described as "beautifully designed," as "sprawling" and "luxurious," as "majestic and serene," as "harmonious" and "elegant." The names of the buildings each contain the word "khiêm," which means "humble" or "modesty."

Today, the mausoleum's mortar is crumbling. The mosaics are cracked and chipped. The walls and roofs sprout vines and shrubbery. The stones erode. The structure suffered some damage in the war, but most of its damage seems to be simply disrepair. To me, it looks like something from many centuries ago, but there are houses in my Ohio township older than the tombs, which were finished two years after the end of the US Civil War, in 1867, making the complex only forty years older than my own home.

It's morning, and we're at a street corner, huddled on stools next to a utility pole dripping with thick black wires, waiting for phở gà, noodle soup with chicken. I'm almost sitting in the road. Motorbike tires whir past as they lean into or out of the turn. It's the last spot available in the crowd of tables. Sweat drips down my back into my shorts. Everyone is slurping up noodles with spoons and chopsticks, tossing their squeezed limes and squares of napkin on the sidewalk, where someone eventually will come and sweep them up. Cris has already eaten one bánh mì sandwich, bought from a cart on the sidewalk, and in a few hours, we'll sit in front of a fan outside a bar on a side street in French Quarter and drink Hà Nội beer while we sweat and watch a young woman in a light summer dress and heels buying oranges from an elderly lady with baskets on a yoke, after which we'll wander a block or so and buy another bánh mì sandwich from another cart.

It's midday, and we feast on fresh shrimp rolls made with rice paper, on tofu rolls, on crepes with shrimp and pork and chicken, on a hot tureen of crab broth. We drink more beer. In the evening, we stroll the streets past bia hơi joints where loud men crowd together over glasses of draft lager. We imagine our next meal.

During its construction, Tự Đức's mausoleum caused him trouble, because of both its cost and the severe treatment of the laborers who were forced to build it. According to one proverb, its walls are made from bones and its trenches filled with blood. One historian tells of a man named Đoàn Trưng who pushed for a coup to replace Tự Đức with his brother Hồng Bảo's son. They attacked the mausoleum, it seems, using mortar pestles, which I have a hard time picturing and is maybe why they didn't succeed. Đoàn Trưng was captured, and the source explains how he was tortured with hot pincers but wouldn't confess even when his thighs were reduced to bare bones. He and his family were beheaded. I try to find more about this story, but no other source mentions the pincers. Another source says that under interrogation, he betrayed Hồng Bảo's son, who was then strangled. This source doesn't say what happened to Đoàn Trưng.

I also try to find out more about Tự Đức's poetry. There are stories of him drinking wine at his lake pavilion and writing poems. Of writing poems with his concubines. Of writing poems to assuage his worries about his ability to govern. Of sipping tea and writing poems. Thousands of poems, the stories say—four thousand, to be exact. I find none of the poems, only mention of them.

We dine on chả cá Lã Vọng, fish cooked with turmeric, dill, and fermented shrimp paste and served with rice noodles, hot chilis, bean sprouts, sliced scallions, and chopped peanuts. A young girl comes over and cuts my noodles with a pair of scissors, as though I'm royalty or, more likely, a child. We drink beer. Back at our hotel, we sip wine, peel the dry skin off longans, revealing the ice-white fruit.

While I can't find any of Tự Đức's poems, I do find poems by another nineteenth-century figure, Nguyễn Công Trứ, a mandarin who held various offices around Việt Nam throughout his life. One poem mourns a life wasted, explaining that a life is only thirty-six thousand days and already the speaker has spent sixteen thousand of these. It asks that the maker turn back time and give the speaker more time to play. Thirty-six thousand days is over ninety-eight years. This number appears in several Vietnamese poems I read, but I don't know where it comes from. Nguyễn Công Trứ lived to be eighty.

One detail in the stories about Tự Đức that sticks with me is his habit of drinking tea made with dew collected from lotus flowers. While his royal army fought French naval shells with inferior weapons and his commanders took their own lives, a servant rowed around the calm lake at the mausoleum and tipped the fat pink blossoms into a pitcher, each drop adding a little, until hundreds of flowers later, there was enough water to boil.

We dine on green papaya salad and squid salad, on stuffed crab, on fried balls of taro. We dine on razor clams, on pumpkin soup, on fruit elaborately carved into birds. We dine on crab asparagus soup and on steamed tuna with pineapple and noodles, which we wrap carefully in rice paper and dip in sauce. We drink beer and wine and lemony sidecar cocktails and, occasionally, tea.

Having lost sovereignty of the Mekong Delta to France, Tự Đức ruled over a country descending into confusion. When the French attacked the citadel in Hà Nội, it fell, and the Vietnamese official in charge hanged himself. The end was near, but nearer for Tự Đức, who died at fifty-four after a reign of thirty-six years. Despite the wives and concubines, he had no children, and thus no one to write his eulogy, and so he wrote his own before his death, which some say was bad luck. The stone stele on which it is inscribed took four years to bring from the north and weighed around twenty tons. The inscription documents his actions and inactions, his regrets and weaknesses. It runs unusually long.

On the sidewalks in Hội An, we eat sour egg drop soup with tapioca and quail eggs, topped with mint and basil, and a very old woman with betel-stained teeth corrects Cris when he adds chilis to his bowl instead of black pepper and then happily mimes the recipe for us. When we ask what the dish is, a younger woman running the stand informs us that it's "soup." In an alley, we eat fat yellow noodles with orange-colored prawns, orange quail eggs, lettuce, fish mint, bean sprouts, broth, and peanuts. A kitten walks by with a slice of red chili on its back. We stop at a cart serving phở with pickled ginger as a condiment, a Japanese influence. The proprietress stands over me, instructively adding chili peppers and fish sauce to my dish, while an elderly man with a puppy playing at his feet teaches Cris how to count. In the market, Cris orders cao lầu, and then somehow through miscommunication also orders a sort of cơm or rice dish, and he sits under the tarp working away at two meals. The first, slices of pork with lettuce, herbs, and fat, square noodles. The second, a bowl of rice topped with water spinach, tofu, carrots, onions, and an enormous chicken leg.

At the markets, we see baskets of brown and white chicken eggs, speckled quail eggs, large greenish duck eggs, baskets of long purple eggplant, loofah, husked coconuts, rough cylinders of cassava. We see piles of bean sprouts, vaguely reminiscent of thin, pale worms. We see a bowl full of hard, brown larvae, which turn out to be silkworms. We see ducklings—fluffy, peeping—and palm-sized pineapples. We see vibrant green limes and tendrils of peas. We see stacks of flat fish, eyes staring blindly at more stacks of fish. In the evening, along the river, we see, over coals burning on the sidewalk, a beast of some sort turning on a spit.

After floating on our backs in the salty sea in the early morning, we return to town and on a side street are served hot bowls of light broth with noodles, tomatoes, bamboo shoots, tofu, and spongy slices of kidney.

We eat sweet pineapple, papaya, guava, sugary jackfruit, rambutans, and persimmons, drink salted lemon juice, watermelon juice, lime juice. We eat the supernaturally pink fruit, which is dragon fruit. Inside, the flesh is white with tiny black seeds that crunch—its flavor, bland.

We dine on chicken soup with egg, on sticky rice wrapped in banana leaves, on glass noodle salad with shrimp, chased with bottles of beer. We dine on five-spice beef, on shaking beef or bò lúc lắc, on prawns wrapped in beef, on mango salad, on pomelo salad with shrimp and toasted rice crackers, on spicy seafood soup with slices of light green okra. We dine on white roses, delicate dumplings made of rice batter and sprinkled with golden fried shallots. We sit on the steps of our bungalow patio a few yards from the shore of the Thu Bồn River, drinking wine and cognac, watching fishermen at dusk work their nets over the water.

In Đà Nẵng, as we wait in the packed station to board our train to Huế, we eat a wedge of crunchy, pear-like fruit offered to us by a stranger, a woman who speaks no English but jokes with me about how tall I am compared to her.

In Huế, we dine on tamarind fish soup, and when I dive in with my chopsticks, I bring up a slab-like steak of white fish. We raise bottles of beer to our lips and swallow hard. We drink wine in a deserted piano bar at our resort, listening to a young girl play American show tunes to a crowd of empty loveseats. We stroll the resort grounds past a drained lotus pond, where women with rubber gloves and brushes scrub at algae. In our room, we drink wine and peel a mango, which tastes of cinnamon, and then bathe in a tub the size of a grave.

Tự Đức had three adoptive sons, and his will asked that his nephew, fourteen-year-old Kiến Phúc, take the throne instead of oldest son Dục Đức, whom he felt was unfit and a bit of a playboy. The regents ignored this request and named Dục Đức emperor. According to one source, Dục Đức continued his ways during the mourning period and slept with Tự Đức's concubines, and so he was forced by the regents to take poison. Another says he was left to starve in confinement. Some say his crime was having Tự Đức's will altered to remove the part about him being unfit to rule, but other sources say this part was read to the court, which is why he was dethroned. Other accounts simply state that he ruled for one day, or three days, or three months. The stories I read of Dục Đức's successors are also varied. Hiệp Hòa made it only a few months, then was forced by the regents to commit suicide for sealing Việt Nam's fate under the French. Kiến Phúc, Tự Đức's original choice for his successor, followed Hiệp Hòa as emperor but died of unknown causes or was poisoned by his adoptive mother after a few months on the throne when he caught her in bed with a regent. What's absolutely clear is that none of them got to build himself a mausoleum to enjoy, having all three died within a year of Tự Đức.

In Huế, we rent bicycles and ride out to Tự Đức's mausoleum, a few miles from our resort. Along the roadside, drying in the sun, spread joss sticks of pungent incense, colored green, yellow, and pink. Inside the giant wall encircling the site, the compound stretches before us, the buildings picturesque in their decay. Tự Đức's sepulcher lies past the courtyard with the statues of mandarins, past the stele pavilion and its obelisks, past a now-dry curved pond, bottom covered in grass. Within a first wall, a second, smaller wall surrounds the tomb, which sits exposed to the weather, a forgettable gray rectangular box. No one lingers at the actual tomb long. There's not much to see.

On our way back to Huế, we try to take a different route and find ourselves on a dirt path elevated above rice paddies. We're alone surrounded by green. A mile or two from Tự Đức's mausoleum, we ride past what looks like another tomb, unmarked, on a grassy slope, with staircases leading to a walled-in space. The sun is setting, and we're lost, so we turn around, leave without looking in. Back at our resort, we sit on our porch drinking cold beer, listening to geckos chirp in the dark.

On our final night in Việt Nam, we roam a dark street in Huế looking for a restaurant that doesn't exist. A dog barks at us through a gate. Bats swoop. No streetlamps shine. At the end of a block, we find an open-air café, dimly lit except for a patio where groups of people ignore the Victoria's Secret fashion show on the television in the corner—young men with dates, a family with a half dozen children. The ground is speckled with napkins, soda cans. The host seems surprised to see us, as if we've arrived late to a party we weren't invited to in the first place, but he's friendly and brings us warm beer and a bucket of ice. Next to a bar decorated with artificial vines, a cook tends a grill, some big section of a body over the coals. He pulls the meat off and slices away. When we ask for whole grilled squid, he sits on a chair next to the grill watching it smoke. The squid is tender and charred and smooth in our mouths. Cris orders chicken, and when it arrives, it's a half a bird, the flesh toward the bone pink. In the morning, for breakfast, I savor my last mango, a fruit I save for the very end of the meal because otherwise everything else tastes dull.

Some say Tự Đức lies in his tomb, but a more prevalent story is that, in the end, Tự Đức wasn't even buried at the mausoleum where he spent sixteen years in luxury. Instead, his resting place is secret, the location of his grave and the treasure he took with him unknown, in the most unknowable way. The two hundred men who buried him were made to keep quiet, which is to say, they were beheaded. His place in his paradise is empty, but can that matter to him now?

fonoteca nacional

memoria de otro tiempo sonora, coyoacán, mexico city

In the two-room exhibit, phonographs and antique radios tease visitors with silence, their labels reading "No tocar." Don't touch. But how else will we wind them up or switch them on, hear the voices lost to the past, the sounds of another time? Huge blossoms of horns tip toward my ears. Curlicue-carved wooden grilles decorate cloth-covered speakers. Curved, wooden art deco cabinets crouch on pedestals. Bakelite and plastic cases, chrome-spangled, hint at brassy broadcasts.

Dials define old radios. Inside, the dial cord winds around a pulley so that twirling the tuner sends the indicator needle along the path of hertz. On the face, the red line slides back and forth, as though reading the mind of the hand on the knob. I've always been mesmerized by this mystery, as I have by the motion of an Etch A Sketch, another machine animated using knobs and pulleys. Years ago, I mastered writing in cursive on the toy's silvery screen, coordinating the vertical and horizontal to move as one.

Fonoteca Nacional resides in a Moorish-influenced rust-red eighteenth-century house, with arches and gates and balconies and courtyards and gardens and fountains, sitting along a quiet street in Coyoacán. In the gardens, mounted loudspeakers along the walkways softly play a soundtrack of a woman singing, so faint I have to linger close to hear. Cats loll atop an expansive pergola among wisteria branches, which are beginning to bloom. On the patio below, dishes for cat food. The house is called Casa Alvarado, though the story that conquistador Pedro de Alvarado lived there is both unproven and odd, since he died in 1541, crushed by a horse.

When I was a kid, my mother kept her Panasonic radio on the kitchen counter. Black and heavy, it had both AM and FM channels, though we mostly listened to AM. Sometimes it played music, the sappily produced songs of 1970s soft rock. Sometimes it announced Milwaukee Brewers games. Sometimes it muttered the news, most of which meant nothing to me, a kind of background noise to my mother's morning or evening routine. Sometimes, on snowy mornings, we willed it to call school cancellations.

But when I think of that radio, what I think of most is Paul Harvey's *The Rest of the Story,* his iconic microprogram featuring supposedly hidden stories in history (some less fact-checked than others), which were digestible by little kids, as each episode was shorter than four minutes long. Though I can't remember many of the specific stories, I can still hear in my head his advertisements for Roach Prufe bug killer. I try to find a recording of these ads but can't seem to track anything down—his emphatic spelling of "P-R-U-F-E" inaccessible through archives.

In 1998 Nobel Prize–winning poet Octavio Paz died while living at

Casa Alvarado. A year before, the apartment where he resided for years had burned, destroying much of his cherished library, and so he and his wife moved to the historic mansion, which the president of Mexico had given to the Paz Foundation. When I listen to a recording of Octavio Paz from 1961, his voice is less deep than I've imagined all these years as I've read his poems. My Spanish is too poor to follow along with his reading. The meaning is lost to me, and all I hear is the cadence of incantation.

Years ago in 2004, I read poems on the radio. On Cleveland's NPR affiliate, WCPN, host Dee Perry ran a show called *Around Noon,* which featured interviews about arts and culture. The show was nerve-wrackingly live, but Dee's low, smooth voice made pointing my mouth at the foam-covered microphone a little less terrifying. The strange thing about being on live radio is that you can never hear yourself as others would. I was given a tape of the show, which I don't remember ever listening to. I'm guessing it's in my attic somewhere, but it may be lost and lost forever, this younger voice of mine, because there aren't archives of *Around Noon* available.

One of the projects of Fonoteca Nacional is to preserve "sonidos en peligro de extinción," or sounds in danger of extinction. These include the sounds of fading Indigenous languages in Mexico, like Kiliwa, spoken by only twenty-nine individuals according to the archive, though some sources say there are even fewer speakers. Also preserved are the sounds of various Mexican animals, including the melodious chirps of two species of frogs, the rana de árbol yucateca and the rana pico de pato, and the purring growls of jaguars and ocelots. But my favorite sounds in the collection are the endangered sounds of oficios, or trades.

One of these trades is the organillero, whose sounds permeate the streets of Mexico City. Uniformed organ grinders churn their heavy and sometimes out-of-tune instruments, producing nostalgic melodies. Less appreciated by younger, ear-budded generations, the organ grinder's soundtrack is sometimes considered more a nuisance than a treasure, and people have been known to pay them to move along out of earshot.

When Octavio Paz died, he left all of his papers and rights to his work to his wife, Marie-José Tramini. For twenty years, she delayed deciding what to do with this collection of unpublished poems, art, letters from famous thinkers and artists and writers—a national treasure worth millions. She distrusted Mexican institutions to care for it properly, even, apparently, the Paz Foundation housed in Casa Alvarado, a building described in one 2001 article as "somewhat crumbling" and in another as "dark, crumbling." She felt she knew best what Paz would've wanted, including not rushing unpublished work to print, but she didn't seem able to act on this intuition. In time, the Paz Foundation would be dissolved and with it the dreams people had of housing Paz's legacy in Casa Alvarado.

I stumbled into Casa Alvarado in 2018 on my third trip to Mexico City. I'd walked past it on a previous visit but hadn't paid it any mind. To be honest, I entered it only to see if they had a restroom I could use, but that meant signing the guest book with the guard at the door, and once inside, I was curious. There were no other visitors and not much indication of what the place was. The exhibit with the radios hadn't yet opened for the day, so I wandered around the garden while I waited. Only later did I learn that this is where Paz died.

My mom still has the radio that sat on the kitchen counter, just as I still have the one-speaker Emerson AM/FM cassette radio I got in grade school, though I can't tune it in to 93.3 WQFM and listen to eighties rock, waiting for my favorite songs to play so I can record them on Maxell tapes, because the station no longer exists. When I took my radio to college, friends made fun of its single speaker and tape deck, this being the era of the stereo CD / cassette / FM radio combo boom box. The hulking black boom box my husband had in college sits in our basement. Why is it hard to get rid of a working radio, even when I never turn it on? I could certainly use it to listen to the news, but the sounds I imagine it speaking are the sounds of the past.

Four months after I visited Casa Alvarado and twenty years after Paz's death, his widow, Marie-José, died, leaving no will and no next of kin. Paz's only daughter had died in 2014, the day before a celebration in honor of the hundredth anniversary of his birth, and Marie-José's only sister and her sister's children died in a plane crash in 1968. Marie-José never decided what to do with Paz's papers and the rights to his work, and she left no instructions. Toward the end of her life, she'd grown extremely isolated and distrustful of others, a recluse. His treasures waited at various residences, including in the burned apartment, which had been unoccupied for years, and in Marie-José's last home, both infested with a squalor of cats. None of his papers had been organized or inventoried. No one knew what was where. Some worried that work could be stolen and sold. Others worried that with no one holding the rights to his work, his poems and essays would go out of print and the legacy of one of Mexico's greatest authors would fade into silence.

Instead, according to Mexican law, in the absence of an heir, a government charity service known as Desarrollo Integral de la Familia, or DIF, has been declared the heir of the estate. The typical work of this agency is providing support for underprivileged families—buying Christmas presents for children, for instance, or walkers for the blind, or housing for the homeless. Not managing a priceless estate of someone like Paz. They'll be able to sell the properties—various apartments owned by the couple—but not the literary artifacts, which will be housed in El Colegio Nacional. A new foundation will oversee the protection of the artifacts of the Paz and Tramini estate, which specialists from Instituto Nacional de Bellas Artes y Literatura are inventorying and assessing for preservation needs (I think of all those cats)—from the cultural, like papers and artwork, to the valuable, like jewelry and oriental rugs, to the mundane, like pots and pans. It will take some time. I imagine someone will have to decide which items are indeed national treasures and artistic monuments and which, like the shoes in the closet, are not worth saving. As someone who has carried an inexpensive old radio to homes in five different states for over almost four decades, I'm certain I'd be bad at this kind of decision-making.

Another trade in the archive of sonidos en peligro de extinción is the camotero, the vendor who sells the traditional snack of hot bananas and sweet potatoes from a three-wheeled wood-fueled oven steered through the streets. The carts have large smokestacks and a steam whistle to announce the cart's arrival to the neighborhood, a sound that pierces through the walls of apartment buildings, letting residents know the camotero is nearby. From a drawer in the oven where the food stays hot, the vendor can pull out a purplish sweet potato, slice it open, and drizzle it with sweetened condensed milk. But this treat is losing popularity to snacks one doesn't have to wait around and listen for, packaged stuff found at any corner store.

On my first visit to Mexico City, in the neighborhood of La Condesa, I heard the whistle one night but didn't know what made the sound. I didn't know I should run down the stairs of the apartment where I was staying and out to the sidewalk to find the sweet source. Instead, I listened, puzzled, as the noise traveled through the shady streets between the art deco buildings. Again and again, growing louder then softer, fading as the camotero moved on, a nameless squeal penetrated the dark.

gall

At my home in Ohio, while trimming branches off two white oak trees by our vegetable garden, I noticed that many of their green leaves had galls, the wart-like protuberances formed by insects on plants. Most of the galls I find are hard knobs, such as the spheroidal growths appearing on the stems of goldenrod, as though the plant swallowed golf balls. But unlike other galls I've seen, which are clearly plant matter, the oak galls seemed like they could be some strange insect larvae—pale-yellow blobs about the size of a gumdrop covered in short magenta hairs. Though I was pretty sure they were galls, I poked one to see if it would move.

These galls are hedgehog galls, and I suppose they could also be cute Japanese anime characters. The insect that makes them is the tiny cynipid wasp *Acraspis erinacei*. The galls got me thinking about the idiomatic use of "gall," as in "Oh! The gall!" Lately, I can't read the news without this phrase buzzing around in my head. It's an ugly word, gall, like the sound of someone gagging, which fits because it means bile. To be bilious is to be nauseated, but also to be spiteful. It's interesting that "bile" became synonymous with ill temper, since it's something we kind of need to digest food. But bile tastes nasty, its bitterness like regret for bad decisions.

171

The hedgehog gall is the product of a female wasp depositing her eggs in oak leaves, which then develop galls around the larvae. Inside each of my hedgehogs are one to eight larvae, growing in the protection of their spiky little ball. In the fall, wasps emerge from the gall, and these wasps are all female. The wasps have two kinds of generations, and this first one is asexual. The second, sexual generation will appear once these females lay parthenogenically produced eggs on the leaf buds; the new eggs create tiny galls on the buds, growths totally different from the hedgehogs on the leaves, from which both female and male wasps emerge in spring and mate so the female can begin the cycle again. An all-female generation upon which the whole process is dependent—I think about this, wondering.

I think also about the name cited again and again in the wasp study I'm reading titled "Review of the World Genera of Oak Cynipid Wasps": Kinsey. As in Alfred Kinsey, sex guy. He wrote his dissertation on cynipids, and I suppose their habits contributed to his interest in ours. Kinsey's 1948 and 1953 reports on male and female sexuality are credited with bolstering both the feminist movement and the fight for LGBTQ+ rights. His conclusions showed that what society said was sexually normal did not reflect how people truly behaved. By putting his information out into public conversation, he helped transform the way people thought about sex and about the roles of men and women.

I examine this gall on the smooth surface of the oak leaf, its pink and yellow pincushion form. When the wasp lays her eggs, she stimulates the oak leaf to react in such a way that it produces the gall. Different cynipids create different kinds of oak galls, and the galls reflect the part of the tree on which they form. *What gall?* One, called the bullet gall, forms a hard ball on twigs. Another, called the jumping gall, forms small bumps on leaves—when the galls fall off, the larvae's movement inside can cause the galls to jump on the ground, like a Mexican jumping bean (which isn't a bean at all but a seed from a shrub with a particular moth larva inside). Exactly how the galls are induced and why they take such shapes is mysterious, buried in molecular messages between the wasp and the oak.

Often when the word "gall" is invading my thoughts in recent days, I'm thinking: *Who are these people? Where did they come from? How can they see the world so differently than I do?*

When I really consider the gall, I realize it isn't on the oak leaf; it *is* the oak leaf. The wasp doesn't produce the gall. It simply introduces elements that affect the way the leaf grows. The oak leaf, inhabited by this other message, transforms itself.

As for the white oaks that bear these galls, I didn't plan to have them next to the vegetable garden—a strange location for shade trees. Years ago, we heeled them in as seedlings until we found a permanent place to plant them. But because they weren't really in the way, we kept forgetting to move them, and now, established, they are part of the landscape.

in harmony with nature

The other day, as I prepared to make some yogurt in my yogurt maker, I noticed that the organic milk I was using said this on the carton: "Produced in harmony with nature." It's true that I'm the kind of person who loves yogurt enough to own a yogurt maker and who buys fancy organic milk. I'm also the kind of person who stands around reading milk cartons.

Because I grew up in Wisconsin—America's Dairyland—I have a nostalgic fondness for both milk cartons and dairy cows, which is why I've been trying to figure out what to make of this claim that the milk in my carton was "produced in harmony with nature." What on earth does that mean? I know well what a dairy farm looks like—giant red barns, multiple navy-blue Harvestore silos or concrete silos with white checkerboard patterns around the top, acres and acres of clovery pasture, fields of corn, enormous rolls of hay, and hundreds of mooing cows. Dairy farms can, in the green of summer, be quite picturesque in a sprawling, cultivated kind of way (though they emit a whiff of cow shit), but they are clearly built for agricultural industry. And dairy cows themselves, when you really look at them, are carefully bred milk-making machines, with enormous udders bulging between oddly delicate hind legs that reach up to pointy rear pin bones and fly-swatting tails. These creatures are no product of Darwinian competition.

Of course, we can argue, and I do, that we are all part of nature, and thus, dairy cows are too—*nature* is such a fluttery term, hard to pin down. I'm not terribly musical, but it seems to me if we're on the same note—nature—we can't really be in harmony, we can only be in unison. But if we think of nature as something "other," something we can be in or out of harmony with, then what does being in harmony with it entail? That question seems a bit big— and fluttery—for me, but another question doesn't: what is "in harmony with nature" selling us, besides fancy milk?

I have my suspicions, and when I start poking around for stuff associated with the phrase, many of the images that pop up on my screen are what I expect. Being in harmony with nature means trees—big trees with arching canopies of glowing green leaves. In several instances, it means creepy tree branches shaped into woody arms with twiggy, bark-covered hands that reach out to shake skin-covered human hands. I try to imagine what the tree and the person are shaking hands about. Maybe they've just met or are cementing a deal. Or perhaps they are saying goodbye.

"In harmony with nature" also seems to mean young white women with long hair sitting on the ground in the lotus position or standing with their arms thrown out in ecstasy. Sometimes the women are in fields of dandelions, sometimes they are next to a body of water. In one forty-five-second stock video a person can purchase titled *Lonely Girl in Harmony with Nature Raises Her Hands Up on a Sandy Beach at Sunset,* the "girl," who appears to be in her twenties, stands in a very short white shirtdress facing what looks like a mudflat. The camera pans back as she indeed raises her hands up, lifting her short hemline just a bit higher, the camera position dropping so we can almost, but not quite, see her loneliness. Then she glances back over her shoulder, tosses her hair, and steps onto the mudflat, come-hither-ish. I look up the portfolio of the creator of this video, and their work includes *Two Silhouettes of Men Climb a Mountain on a Steep Slope at Sunset,* which is exactly what is sounds like; *People in Dining Room,* where hands holding tongs reach for glop in steam trays; and a bunch of videos of paper currency being counted by machines. I also find a whole series of videos involving the lonely girl on the beach, where she's described in various ways, depending on what she's doing—cheerful, barefoot, flirting, sad, dancing, and sexy— though each is essentially filmed in the same spirit as the lonely girl clip. A vast range of emotions can be projected onto a young woman in a short dress on a beach at sunset, including "in harmony with nature."

What I didn't expect to find associated with the phrase "in harmony with nature" were dozens of real-estate advertisements for luxury homes. It's not like this is a catch-all phrase for any house with a nice view, either, because it seems to be hinged only to houses that clearly overstep their environmental footprint. In an article from *Christie's International Real Estate* titled "Luxury Living: Homes in Harmony with Nature," the descriptions of the five domiciles feature amenities like a swimming pool, guest house, staff cottage, and working stud farm with forty-three stables. The homes themselves include a ten-bedroom chateau, a 6,489-square-foot "mountain retreat," a "stately manor house," a "seafront villa in a protected conservation area," and a $17,500,000 "luxury compound" in Idaho so enormous that this "modern mountain home" could be captured only through an aerial photo depicting eighteen acres of grounds with a pool, driveways, and clusters of buildings embedded in a protected area that is "habitat for moose and bald eagle." Again and again, I find luxury properties worldwide—

including one complete with a free gas-powered Honda Civic—that someone wants the world to believe are "in harmony with nature."

"In harmony with nature" seems to be selling us dreams. Specifically, it seems to be selling us the dream that the world loves us and all the stuff that comes with us.

When I think about harmony, I think about the few years I spent singing alto in high school choir. Unlike the soprano lines, tumbling along the melody, the alto parts I performed tended to be bland. For instance, I remember soaring sopranos belting out their angelic announcement in the "Hallelujah" chorus from Handel's *Messiah,* while we altos never ranged far from an endless series of A notes. But it turns out, those boring As are essential to the harmony. Some part has to be steady and predictable for the angels to pull off what they do.

And what is harmony? I generally think of harmony as a chord made up of notes that create a pleasing effect. "Pleasing," of course, seems subjective. But not all harmonies are considered "pleasing." There are both consonant harmonies—the "pleasant" sort—and dissonant harmonies, which many ears find unpleasant. Consonant harmonies have stability and make us feel good, while dissonant harmonies are unstable and make us feel uneasy. John Williams plays around with dissonance in his movie soundtracks, so hearing these harmonies may evoke sharks, aliens, or heavy-breathing former Jedi knights. That said, one study involving native Amazonians in Bolivia seems to show that "pleasant" is indeed subjective, and that exposure to Western culture may be the factor in deciding how we react to consonant and dissonant harmonies.

I'm left wondering what kind of harmony my milk is engaged in with nature, which seems more complicated than the harmony of the lonely girl and luxury houses. I contact the local grocery chain that sells the milk under its own brand to see where it comes from, and it turns out it's Organic Valley milk, a national brand, but marketed with the store's label. Organic Valley's promo material says that its farms are "pastoral, low-stress environments" with an average herd size of seventy-eight cows. Their website features lots of cute videos of Holsteins and Guernseys and Jerseys and Brown Swiss frolicking in organic pastures. Organic Valley is a co-op of farmers. I find that several farms in the co-op are within an hour of my house, including Mast Dairy and Stoney Bottom's Farm (which should not be confused with Stoney Bottom Farm, a California producer of craft cannabis).

On a mostly cloudy July afternoon, with storms threatening, I decide to take a short road trip south to check out the two dairies. Will there be frolicking cows, happy and harmonious? The country roads are lined with green corn and hayfields and century farms, as well as double-wide ranch houses. Rural northeast Ohio isn't the kind of nature in the "harmony with nature" pictures— no beaches or mountains or even very many huge trees to shake hands with. At one point along the way, a deer leaps from some woods and bolts across the shady road, but I also pass a lot of fake deer statuary planted in front yards keeping company with wishing wells and glider swings. This isn't the suburbs, so the landscaping isn't what one might call manicured. Tastes lean more toward petunias in tractor tires.

I pass many signs in yards for a service called "Guard My Yard Pest Control." I also pass a sign in one yard that reads "Stop the Brine," a reference, I assume, to the region's hydraulic fractur-

IN HARMONY WITH NATURE • 179

ing industry and its injection wells. I'm curious if the antifracking movement is as strong here as the antipest sentiment. Fracking has been under scrutiny for damage ranging from polluting drinking water near the wells to causing earthquakes, and the trucks that carry the brine are a loud and ubiquitous presence around injection-well sites. Then there's the brine itself. Some Ohio legislators would like to approve the use of such brine as a deicing agent on roads, despite tests conducted by the Ohio Department of Natural Resources on one injection-well, brine-based product, AquaSalina, that found the brine contained levels of radium three hundred times higher than that allowed in drinking water. In its promotional material, the company that makes AquaSalina, Nature's Own Source, touts the fact that it's produced from "natural resources, not freshwater," and so saves fresh water when compared to other deicers. What they mean by "natural resources" is confusing to me, as is the meaning of the company's name. Is nature providing a product from an unnamed source? Or is the product the source—the origin—of nature, like cows are milk's own source?

As I drive farther south, the aesthetic shifts to the tidy white houses of the Amish, laundry dangling from clotheslines strung via pulley system to the tops of barns. At one house, it's clearly dark-blue-pants-washing day, with dozens of legs hanging. At another, a wall of pale sheets flap along the line. I can tell which houses are Amish by the curtains, uniformly white and tied back in perfect symmetry, like a child's drawing of curtains. Two girls in blue dresses roll by pushing scooters, carrying in their scooter baskets blocks of ice wrapped in clear plastic. They wave. I pass a small schoolhouse with some seesaws and a pair of outhouses. Various businesses appear along the road. Though this isn't what one would call a town, it clearly is a community, each enterprise embracing its own entrepreneurial niche—selling boots, fabric, vegetables, AKC puppies, rabbits, pies. And among these somewhere, organic milk.

My GPS tells me I've reached my destination, Stoney Bottom's Farm, but the building in front of me isn't a green pasture with frolicking Guernseys. It looks more like a warehouse from a small industrial park. To one side are wooden pallets piled as high and wide as the building. Pallet making is one of the wood-oriented niches of the Amish, along with manufacturing things like furniture, flooring, and custom cabinets and molding. From inside the building, I hear the squeal of power saws. The operation is clearly part of a large family farm, which consists of several houses and lots of outbuildings. A few rust-colored chickens peck around in the yard, where some children play. I try to spy beyond the main compound area, behind the houses, past a line of trees. There's pasture back there, and I can make out vague white blobs, but the cows are too far away for me to hear them mooing, in harmony or not.

I drive on to Mast Dairy, which doesn't yield clearer results. In fact, I'm not sure I even know which farm it is along the hilly road. Green field runs into green field, and I can't see any house numbers. No signs advertise the dairy, unlike my first-grade teacher Mrs. Dalton's dairy farm in Wisconsin, which had "Daltondale" written in big letters across the barn. I do see—again far from the road—a few Holsteins standing around, but I can't tell by looking at them whether or not their milk is organic.

I'm certain I couldn't tell if the milk was organic even by tasting it. I'm not a big connoisseur of the stuff, only buying it to make my beloved yogurt. I've never been a fan of a big glass of milk and had to be goaded into drinking it when I was a kid (unless, of course, it was chocolate milk). Though I love cheese and ice cream, I try not to think much about the milk itself, how we make an animal create for us on schedule, twice a day, what it would normally be feeding its offspring, hooking it up to machines that perform a probably less pleasant imitation of what a calf does.

Cows don't exist in the wild on this continent, unless you count their bison cousins. But if wild cows did exist, and we somehow milked them, would we be their parasites? (No one in their right mind would milk a bison. According to the National Bison Association, "the females do not adapt well to the type of handling necessary in a milking operation.") It seems to me we certainly would be, squeezing them of their protein and calcium and tasty fats. And is a parasite—like a deer tick or a guinea worm—in harmony with its host, living side by side, measure by measure, in the same composition until the inevitable coda?

I consider the packages of lactobacillus bacteria (imported from Bulgaria—*fancy*) I add to my milk to make my yogurt, which in turn inhabit my own gut, helping me digest food, boosting my immune system, and all the other stuff hawkers of probiotics purport. One maker of over-the-counter probiotic supplements, Align, describes the relationship between these bacteria and my gut as "symbiotic." Are my bacteria and I living in harmony, at least until a bad infection forces me to take antibiotics that will wipe them out?

Cows, too, have a gut microbiome full of beneficial bacteria, but also fungi, protozoa, and a kind of organism called archaea. Cows digest the cellulose in grass and hay, which we can't, and this array of internal helpers makes that possible. But the byproduct of digesting cellulose is methane, a greenhouse gas that contributes to global climate change. In an attempt to reduce greenhouse gas emissions by cows, scientists are working on several solutions, including creating a vaccine targeted against the archaea most responsible for methane production and breeding cows who produce less methane. Methane itself is created through natural processes in the cow, so are these less methaney cows more in harmony with nature or just less responsible for climate change? Can the quality of "harmony" even be measured in terms of more or less?

When I hear the word "symbiosis," I think of the flower and the bee, both benefiting from the relationship they have to each other. But it turns out that parasitism is also a form of symbiosis, which simply means "a living together." Symbiotic relationships can be broken down into three basic categories: mutualism, commensalism, and parasitism. The flower/bee relationship is one of mutualism, whereas the relationship between epiphytic plants like orchids and their hosts, in which one species benefits and the other is unaffected, constitutes commensalism. And then there is parasitism, in all its various forms, including that taken by the braconid wasp, which lays its eggs under a hornworm caterpillar's skin, where the larvae develop and begin eating their host's insides until they gnaw through to the outside, form tiny white pupae on the skin, and eventually emerge as wasps. The caterpillar fares poorly in this symbiotic process.

One could think of our relationship with the dairy cows as mutualism, since without our milking them, they would cease to exist. No one would go through the trouble and expense of keeping dairy cows if they weren't going to milk them. They're unlikely pets, despite their sweet cow eyes, and expensive—as illustrated by the number of Wisconsin dairy farms that folded in 2018 alone (around seven hundred)—even with profits from milk. If the United States decided we would no longer milk any cows and released all 9.3 million of them to, say, a dairy cow preserve somewhere to frolic, I imagine predators would make quick work of them, if the cows didn't starve first. But if cows ceased to exist, then they also wouldn't need us anymore, and their part in the composition would be reduced to silent rests.

So why are dairy farms folding? Because of a glut of milk caused, in part, by government programs that encouraged farmers to increase production, by recent tariffs and politics that have affected trade with China and Mexico for the United States' milk, and in 2020, by supply chains interrupted by COVID-19. As the pandemic closed schools and restaurants, which are big consumers of milk, and shut down processing plants, some dairies found themselves dumping milk, and others sold their dairy cows for slaughter as the demand for beef rose.

Today's milk cows also simply produce a lot more milk than cows of yesteryear due to breeding and better feed. You can't just stop milking a cow when prices are poor or demand is low, especially if you've invested a great deal in your farm. In this case, are the cows themselves parasites, sucking the farmers dry, chewing them from the inside out?

Industrial dairy farms have also pushed smaller family farms out of the market and contributed to the overabundance of milk. The name for farms with over seven hundred cows (and others like them that raise chickens and pigs) is Concentrated Animal Feeding Operations, a term which lacks the alliterative musicality of "family farms." Their scale allows them to run more cheaply, and now large-scale CAFOs—those milking over 1,000 cows—produce more than half of the milk in the United States. Around 35 percent of that milk comes from farms with over 2,500 cows.

Initially, some family farms turned to producing organic milk to combat falling milk prices, but then CAFOs also began producing organic milk, and now some sources estimate around half of the organic milk sold in the United States is produced by CAFOs. Big retailers, like Walmart and Costco, prefer to buy their organic milk from large industrial farms and market it under their own brands. Whether this milk is truly organic is questionable, given the standards that must be met for organic milk. For instance, cows must have at least 120 days of grazing time in pasture each year, as well as year-round access to the outdoors. Investigations by the *Washington Post* in 2016 suggest that some of these CAFOs are probably cheating the standards, shorting the required grazing time and feeding the cows mainly through feedlots instead. Given the logistics, I have a hard time picturing the fifteen thousand happy Holsteins on one CAFO featured in the *Post*'s article frolicking together on rolling hills of plentiful green grass. It's also hard for me to imagine the 1.725 million pounds of cow shit those fifteen thousand animals produce daily blending harmoniously with nature.

Another Wisconsin industry that has suffered a bust is the mining of what is called northern white sand. Northern white sand is known as frac sand and is used in the fracking process. Wisconsin happens to have a lot of it lying underneath its lovely hills. During the boom years for sand, companies approached dairy farmers, wanting to buy their sand-rich land and turn it into mines. Some farmers, suffering from dairy prices, sold, and the rural landscape of parts of Wisconsin was transformed from green farms of mooing cows to exposed sand mines, loud with machinery and cloudy with dust. Some farmers who didn't sell found themselves neighbors to ravaged land, unrecognizable from the community where their families had farmed, sometimes for generations.

But the sand-boom years of less than a decade ago have ended, as fracking operations choose to use lesser-quality sand from mines closer to big well sites in Texas and Oklahoma. One analyst has suggested that 75 percent of the mines could close. Bad news for the companies that invested in building the mines. If you can't sell milk, living together with a bunch of cows doesn't do you much good, and the same goes for unprofitable mines. But the news is worse for the land itself, which can't regrow the hills that were suddenly erased in the name of brief profit.

The more I think about harmony—consonant or dissonant—and symbiosis, our lives together in all their forms, the more it seems impossible, as notes on the same score, to *not* be in harmony with nature. Whether the "Hallelujah" chorus or the theme from *Jaws,* a virgin forest or a frac-sand mine, it's all still harmony and living together. So if our being in harmony with nature and all it entails—cows, trees, mudflats, mansions, farms big and small, shale formations rich in natural gas, ice, buried dunes of sand, perhaps even nature's own source—is inherent and inevitable, it seems to me that the question isn't, "What does it mean to be in harmony with nature?" but instead what kind—and length—of song we want our composition to be.

steel

products of cleveland

"As a distant planet was destroyed by old age . . ."
—*Action Comics* no. 1, 1938

He heaves the automobile into a glowing sky, headlight popping off, bumper succumbing, windshield bursting, white rubber tire hurtling away. Machines beware of this force. The automobile is green. Bad guys shudder. The future runs faster than an express train.

The plant is mostly shuttered. If I could get any closer, I could say more about its inaction, but I'm lost on its periphery, above the valley that holds it. The bridge on the map is a road ending in a concrete barrier and chain-link fence. On the other side of the chain-link fence is a chain-link gate, open. Beyond the gate, the asphalt sprouts a Russian olive bush, bright weeds, a green beer bottle. The road crumbles off a cliff. Far below, a rail yard. At the brink, on the road's surface, someone has spray-painted, in white, something that seems to read PUSH.

He runs along the power lines, bad guy in tow. A landscape of skyscrapers leans over him. He knows birds sit on wires and aren't electrocuted. He can joke about this with the bad guy. He can put things into perspective. Far below, automobiles speed by—so small, just tiny boxes.

Past the rails, the plant waits. Looking through the chain link, I can't say how big it is. No one moves down there for scale. It appears bigger than I can really imagine. The buildings loom like nightmares of buildings. Or maybe just very sad, confusing dreams. If I broke it down, I'd call the parts roofs, smokestacks, conveyors, wires, docks, pipes, scaffolding, vents. Inside there must be machines. Surely, though, these aren't the right terms.

The dam cracks farther, pressure building over the town below. But first there's the weakened railroad trestle to attend to, to lift into place until the train passes. Then he lets the trestle crash so he can reach the dam, keep it from collapsing until the people escape to safer ground. But the dam won't hold for long, the irresistible flood escaping. His solutions are temporary. He topples a mountain peak to divert the waters. The town is saved.

Behind the plant, hazy, the tops of the city's tallest buildings poke into grayness—beaux arts to brutalist. On Terminal Tower, a bird rests, ready to dive off a ledge, reaching speeds of two hundred miles per hour. This kind of dive is called the "stoop." Under the tower, trains come and go in tunnels. The trains move slower than the birds, which are falcons.

The bad guys throw her out the window, and she falls, falls, her shadow falling with her on the building's face. Her dress floats up her legs. She falls, toes pointed in red heels, lovely in her falling. But he sees her, springs into the air, cradles her in his arms. She still feels like she is falling.

In courtship, the peregrine falcon dives and swoops. Sometimes the male brings prey to the female in flight, passing the food in his talons as she flies upside down, like the belly-to-belly mirror formation fighter planes execute at air shows. I imagine it this way, anyhow. From the edge of the missing bridge, I can't see the bird.

The patient from the asylum makes his way out onto the building's ledge. He wants to end it all, a moment of pain followed by nothingness. He jumps. Can he be saved? Of course he can.

The plane that flies inverted is always number five. The number five painted on the plane is inverted, as is the number five on the pilot's uniform.

The moment the trigger is pulled, he fires himself into motion, racing so fast we can't even see him. But we know it happens because there he is, his body blocking the boy, bullet bouncing off his chest, as though his insignia were the target and was always meant to be.

Another tower belongs to the Justice Center, a grid of concrete and windows. Inside, courtrooms full of arguments. It is the center of justice, like a sun or black hole, pulling criminals into the orbit of consequences. Here is the Police Museum, with its artifacts of crime. I've seen there the death masks of unidentified victims of dismemberment, their painted faces calm, unastounded. The murders, never solved, cease in 1938. Outside, a sculpture titled *Portal,* which looks like ductwork.

He finds the man in quicksand, sucked up to his torso, so he pulls, wrestles the grip of the quagmire so hard he almost tears the man apart. But his strength prevails, and he hauls the man out, step by step, the quicksand resisting. As he reaches solid ground, bloodhounds lunge. He always has his hands full.

If I gazed down from the sky, I could see a ghost bridge, the line the mind draws over the valley between two disconnected roads. Across from the missing bridge rise the sooty spires of the church of Saint Michael the Archangel.

Against a backdrop of moon, his caped figure hurries, silhouetted, face erased by darkness. He must awaken the governor. The governor generally sleeps through everything.

If I were to turn away from the valley and walk a mile or so, heading toward the lake, I'd come to where they find some of the bodies, in Kingsbury Run. They are poor and headless. Apparently, no one worries about them or at least misses them. The famous safety director worries about them, but he worries too late.

He sits on his bed, wearing only his drawers. His hat, his white shirt beside him, his jacket slung over a chair. He lingers between identities.

In the shantytowns of Kingsbury Run, the working poor wear jackets and hats, shirts with collars. They heat coffee in pots on stoves, the inside furnishings outside. A dog sits on an upholstered chair in the midst of debris. Two investigators disguise themselves as hoboes, carry their belongings on the end of a stick. This is how to survive a depression.

He smashes the bad guys' oil well. They've been selling worthless stock. Oil spews into the sky. He topples the derrick. He sets fire to the oil. The workers in overalls try to stop him, but he warns them away, yells at them to run for their lives. The workers aren't bad guys. Black smoke curls around the well. He does a thorough job.

Bodies turn up near the shanties. Three men gaze into a metal bucket, one man wearing what appears to be surgical attire, a white smock, white pants. The other two have white hats, brims obscuring their features. Inside the bucket lie bones. Police display a victim's death mask at an exposition, but a hundred thousand people don't know who it is. Detectives x-ray some of the heads. The famous safety director has the shanties burned to the ground, flames revealing nothing but darkness.

He must stop the robbery, so he takes a short cut through the fair's fireworks display, fiery bursts illuminating his suit, a treat for the spectators.

The missing bridge was closed decades ago and demolished—trusses removed, trestle detonated. When built in 1912, it was the longest span in the country. An old illustrated postcard depicts people on the bridge gazing down below. Automobiles cross. Farther away, the vague shape of a horse. In the distance, the bridge disintegrates. The missing bridge is named the Clark Avenue Bridge.

He holds the suspension cables of the bridge, the arched supports crumbling, the deck wavering. It's not clear if he's tearing the bridge to pieces or keeping it together. It's not part of any story, just a demonstration.

If I were to turn away from the plant and walk fifty or so blocks east, I would be standing in front of a two-story duplex next to a sausage shop. Inside, a man has murdered a woman or is about to murder a woman. It's not his first time, or even his second, or third, or fourth, etc. I wouldn't know this standing outside the house. No one knows this. Only in the future do we know this.

The mayor has infuriated him, not enforcing traffic laws and breaking them himself, zipping down the road, speedometer reading ninety. He kidnaps the mayor and carries him to the morgue. Bodies lie under sheets, the suggestion of a face draped in white, victims of accidents.

When alive, the murdered women hidden in the house suffered from poverty and addiction. The women who haven't yet been murdered suffer from poverty and addiction, move from place to place. They're lost. Some have been reported missing by family worried about them. Months later, the police will find bodies in the living room and graves in the basement, in the crawl space, in the backyard. They'll find a skull in a bucket.

The train he's on has missed its signal. It barrels toward an oncoming train. He must help, but he has no time to strip off his outer garments. It doesn't matter. The cape means nothing. In his suit and necktie, he slows the train, braces against both engines, pins himself between, brings them to a stop. Then he disappears before anyone can identify him.

I leave the missing bridge. There must be a way down below, and if I follow the ridge, maybe I'll discover it. I may be trespassing, though I don't see any gates. Industrial detritus riddles the ridge. Dumpsters, fences, and many tires—tires whose usefulness has abandoned them. The road dead-ends at a cul-de-sac. If I perch on a pile of gravel at the lip of the ridge, I can almost touch a stream of power lines swooping down into the valley, each line thick as my wrist.

He saves the train from the washed-out rails, one leg in the river, one arm holding back the streamlined engine. Was there a flood? What swept away the rails? It isn't part of the story. He doesn't need both hands to stop disasters.

A security truck pulls into the cul-de-sac, rolls down its window, a uniformed man inside. I tell him I want to see the plant but can't find my way. He says the plant spans 1,200 acres. He says his shift would be busier in a graveyard. He says he's worked here thirty-nine years. He says he has no pension, no insurance. He says when he leaves, he leaves with the shirt on his back. He says falcons nest on the plant.

He grasps a bad guy under one arm and propels himself from rooftop to rooftop. The bad guy tries to stab him, which messes up his timing. He slams into a building, the two of them falling, falling. He grabs a windowsill with one hand, but the bad guy grabs nothing, doomed. The bad guy hits the sidewalk—little puffs of dust rising—gets what he deserves.

The first headless torso is found where a road dead-ends at Kingsbury Run. I try to find this spot, but it's missing. Where the road should be, a bridge arcs over a railway. The bridge is closed, concrete barriers blocking passage. Behind a fence, cranes with giant magnets sort through piles of scrap. On the other side of the closed bridge, a splintered bureau with a mirror lies on the ground, looking like it's been dropped from a great height. Nearby, a tree with a tire swing, a boarded-up building with sign reading "Quality Saw."

The cab racketeers smash their own cars with sledgehammers. They have no choice. He makes them do it. He threatens to kill them. It might be an idle threat—who knows?

The falcon on the tower will die. He will crash into a building fighting another male. A woman will find his body on the sidewalk. She'll notice his banded leg and call a number. She'll rush him to help, though he's dead and there's no need to rush. The city will mourn. But right now, no one knows this.

He's intrigued. The police are overcome with poisonous gas, and the bad guy escapes. It seems too clever for a common bad guy. There must be someone else behind it, a mastermind. Someone with imagination. Let's see what he can find.

In 1937 the plant workers strike for higher wages, better conditions. They sit down at their machines so no scabs can take their place. The famous safety director threatens to clear the area of picketers. The employers use tear gas. The governor sends in troops to break up the strike. In a few years, the war will come, and everyone will get along.

He spots a dark cabin. Bad guys hide in cabins. Sure enough, inside are bad guys. One is the mastermind, seated in a chair, wearing a white smock.

I'm lost in a graveyard, circling and circling. Obelisks point to the sky. Mausoleums line the shores of ponds like eternal shanties. Urns, crypts, lambs, vaults, angels, tombs, headstones, crosses. A hundred thousand dead. Some died tragically—a president shot, children burned in a school, a shortstop killed by a pitch. I'm looking for a plaque that marks the place where the famous safety director's ashes were scattered. Instead, I stumble on a big dam holding water back.

He gets tossed around a little by the mastermind's henchmen. First electrocution. Then he's strapped to a table with a spinning saw blade. He's fine, though. The saw shatters on his skull, a shard flying off, piercing a bad guy's throat. The mastermind flees by plane, but not for long.

The graveyard calls the dead "residents," and, indeed, they do remain behind, confined to their stories. We know who they are.

He destroys the plane's propeller, sending it hurtling toward earth. A sickening crash, plane blasting into indiscernible parts. But in the wreck, he finds no trace of the mastermind. Is this the end of the mastermind's plan to control the planet? We don't know. We never know.

If I could leap great distances, I could take off at the graveyard, soar two miles, heading north-northwest. I'd land in front of a two-story house, down the street from some boarded-up homes, their faces giving in to gravity. Someday, more plywood sheets will be nailed up to keep out people stealing pipe, wire, scrap to sell. But it's hard to say which houses, which windows. Who is like God? This is a rhetorical question.

Just before the doomed planet explodes into fragments, the scientist places his infant son in an experimental rocket ship. When the vessel reaches our planet, an elderly couple finds the child. "The poor thing!" says the woman. "It's been abandoned."

The security man drives in disbelief around and around the empty plant. The stories he could tell. He knows each building by name. He remembers the missing bridge. What next? The plant will once again fire up its blast furnaces, manufacture clouds in a clear sky, but as I watch white gulls take off and land on railways, on piles of ore, on vacant roads, I don't know this. And in the future, when I see the exhaust of flames escape the furnace, what other futures won't I yet know?

His foster parents tell him to hide his strength or he'll scare people. They tell him when the time comes, he must use it to assist
humanity. When he stands at their graves, grieving, his determi-
nation grows. He becomes what he must.

Who is like El? A young man sits in the attic room of the two-story
house. He is someone with imagination. He writes stories with his
best friend, an artist whose eyes are failing even as he begins to
sketch. They are awkward and isolated. They will never burst the
chains around their chests. They won't get what they deserve, but
no one knows this. Only in the future do we know this. For now,
the future is their creation.

He can hurdle skyscrapers, leap an eighth of a mile, raise tremendous weights, run faster than a streamlined train. Nothing less
than a bursting shell can penetrate his skin. He can crush steel
with his bare hands. Someday, he will fly. Someday, he will turn
back time. It is 1938, and soon it will be tomorrow.

acknowledgments

Thank you to the publications where versions of these essays originally appeared:

Bennington Review: "In Harmony with Nature"
Blood Orange Review: "Patas"
Broad Street: "Project Monarch" (as "A Curious Migration")
Confrontation Magazine: "The Galápagos Shooting Gallery"
Creative Nonfiction: "The Collection"
Fifth Wednesday Journal: "Cage"
Florida Review: "Paradise, Earth"
Flyway: Journal of Writing and Environment: "Hatch"
Fourth Genre: "In the Classroom"
Grist: "The Box"
Mid-American Review: "Zoo World"
Terrain.org: "Songs of the Humpback Whale"
West Branch: "Steel: Products of Cleveland"
"The Collection" was also included in the anthology *Creating Nonfiction: Twenty Essays and Interviews with the Writers,* edited by Jen Hirt and Erin Murphy (SUNY Press, 2016).

Thank you to the Ohio Arts Council for Individual Excellence Awards for creative nonfiction in 2014 and 2020, which supported the writing of this book. Thank you to my colleagues for your flexibility and encouragement and to Hiram College for providing funds for travel and research over the years. Thank you to my wonderful writer friends in Ohio and beyond; you are the best community for support and inspiration. Thank you to the editors at the journals in which some of these essays first appeared, who with care, thought, and patience made them better pieces. Thank you to artist Polly Morgan (pollymorgan.co.uk) for permission to use the image of her sculpture *Today I Wore* (2022) on this book's cover and to Lissi Sigillo for creating the cover design. Thank you to Kristen Elias Rowley and the rest of the kind folks at The Ohio State University Press / Mad Creek Books and *The Journal* Non/Fiction Prize for the hard work of getting words into the world, including these. Special thanks to Elizabeth Zaleski for such wise and thorough untangling of my muddled sentences and for expertly polishing my pages.

Thank you to Michelle Herman for giving this book a spine, a body, a beating heart. Thank you to my aunt, Rebecca Ditgen, who has always made research sound fun. Thank you to my siblings, Heather Ostergren and Paul Quade, who are both inclined to turn over a rock to see what's under it, and their families, who share their curiosity about the world: John, Liz, Mary, Charlie, Penelope, and Phoebe. Thank you to my mom and dad, Judy and Ken Quade, whose own adventures and care for nature inspire me to play outside. Thank you to my traveling companion near and far and through this life in love, Cris Harris.

And thank you to the many people I've met around the planet who have been generous and gentle with this bumbling, introverted stranger—for the ride, the bowl of soup, the slice of fruit, the piece of cheese, the cup of tea, the map and set of directions, the suggestion, the use of your bathroom, the photograph, the laughter or the empathy when I needed one or the other, the pen and paper, the washing machine, the history lesson, the invitation, the shared joke, the gift of a scarf, of a bracelet, of a conversation, of a blessing, of an amulet that I still carry with me.

notes

HATCH

I began the first draft of this essay on June 4, the day I was handed the duckling in the kitchen, so all information about *Deepwater Horizon* was in the news at the time.

The study "Half-Awake to the Risk of Predation," about ducks sleeping with half of their brain still active, appeared in *Nature* on February 4, 1999, and is authored by Niels C. Rattenborg, Steven L. Lima, and Charles J. Amlaner.

Numerous places reported on Dawn dish soap being used for the *Deepwater* oil spill bird rescue, including the *New York Times* in Leslie Kaufman's "Ad for a Dish Detergent Becomes Part of a Story," published June 15, 2010, which also discusses the uncertainty of bird survival after cleaning.

THE COLLECTION

There are various versions of the Nicene Creed. The one I use appeared in the *Lutheran Book of Worship* used by the Evangelical Lutheran Church of America in the 1970s.

The explanation for the scratched-out eyes in the frescoes was something I heard guides mention and read about in guidebooks, such as the *Moon Spotlight Cappadocia* guidebook by Jessica Tamtürk, which states that some of the frescoes "were badly marred during the Byzantine Iconoclastic decade during the 8th century A.D., while most of the eyes were gouged Muslim locals out of fear of the evil eye." This detail certainly piqued my curiosity, but these sources didn't tell me anything more about this practice.

The longer version of the Saint Barbara story I refer to is from *The Golden Legend,* compiled by Jacobus de Voragine in the mid-thirteenth century.

PROJECT MONARCH

The study about pokeweed's antiviral protein is "Pokeweed Antiviral Protein, a Ribosome Inactivating Protein: Activity, Inhibition and Prospects" by Artem V. Domashevskiy and Dixie J. Goss, published January 28, 2015, in the journal *Toxins.*

The website for Western Illinois University's Alternative Crops Research program suggests growing milkweed as a fiber source (among other things) and mentions the use of its floss in life jackets in World War II. It also explains that the floss is hypoallergenic and has a higher thermal rating than down.

The estimate of 240 million acres of historical tallgrass prairie appears in many resources about tallgrass prairies. The National Park Service provided the statistic that 1 percent of historical North American prairie exists today. The Iowa Prairie Network states that 0.1 percent of Iowa prairie remains. The Minnesota Department of Natural Resources created the map of historical versus present-day prairies and provided the number 18 million acres of historical prairie in the state.

Catalina Trail's story appeared in Monika Maeckle's article "Founder of the Monarch Butterfly Roosting Sites in Mexico Lives a Quiet Life in Austin, Texas," published July 10, 2012, on the Texas Butterfly Ranch website.

Butterflies are hard to count, but scientists try. In a news release dated May 24, 2022, the Center for Biological Diversity reported the eastern monarch population has declined 85 percent since the mid-1990s. MonarchWatch.org publishes the yearly butterfly count, which is measured by the number of hectares covered at the wintering grounds in Mexico. The total rises and falls but has reached over 7.2 acres only three times between 2009–10 and 2021–22, peaking at almost 15 acres in 2018–19. This system of measuring isn't perfect because it's not certain how many butterflies are in a hectare (estimates used have ranged from 10–50 million, according to Journey North), nor are other systems used to gather data on butterfly populations. A July 10, 2022, article by Jason Bittel in *National Geographic*, "Monarch Butterflies May Be Doing Better Than Thought, Controversial Study Suggests," discusses the challenges of butterfly counts in the United States and conclusions drawn from these data.

Bruce Stanley reported news of the Vietnamese rhino's rediscovery after it was thought extinct from the effects of war in a June 21, 1993, Associated Press article titled "Scientists Find Surviving Members of Rhino Species." BBC reporter Mark Kinver posted news of the rhino's (final) extinction on October 25, 2011, in the article "Javan Rhino 'Now Extinct in Vietnam.'"

Information on crop acreage and percentage of herbicide-tolerant crops is provided by the US Department of Agriculture Farm Service Agency and Economic Research Service, respectively. The numbers I include for crop acreage are for the 2021 growing season. The percentage of herbicide-tolerant crops reflect data last updated in July 2020. I calculated 163 million acres of herbicide-tolerant land from these figures.

My understanding of the ejidos and ejidatarios comes from my conversations with Ellen Sharp and Joel Moreno, to whom I owe much of what I know about monarchs in Mexico. You can read more about the complications of this system and other obstacles to preserving the wintering grounds in Ellen's powerful and vivid essay "Suspension of Flight," published at *Terrain.org* on April 7, 2022.

The article "Weed Management in the Era of Glyphosate Resistance," written by Mark Jeschke, discusses the dangers of overreliance on glyphosate and appears on the Pioneer company website. Pioneer is part of Corteva Agribusiness, which itself is a spinoff of DowDuPont, as I understand things. The name "Corteva," according to a DowDuPont press release about the company's creation, is a combination of "heart" and "nature" and, I presume, not intended to sound like that of a supervillain.

The press release I mention from the USDA is titled "USDA Launches New Conservation Effort to Aid Monarch Butterflies," dated November 12, 2015.

The numbers reported for the 2020–21 season appear in Mark Stevenson's article for the Associated Press titled "Monarch Butterflies Down 26% in Mexico Wintering Grounds," dated February 25, 2021.

After my first visit in 2015 to the Monarch Butterfly Biosphere Reserve, Ellen Sharp and Joel Moreno established a nonprofit organization, Butterflies and Their People, which hires local people as full-time arborists to monitor the forest of Cerro Pelón and keep an eye on illegal logging. You can learn more about that work on the organization website: https://butterfliesandtheirpeoplemx.org/.

SONGS OF THE HUMPBACK WHALE

I assume an average length of thirty-nine feet for a seventy-two-passenger school bus and fifty feet for a female humpback whale.

The Gerard Manley Hopkins quote is from the poem "Pied Beauty."

Several sources stated that the *National Geographic* flexi disc was the largest single pressing of recording ever, including "'It Always Hits Me Hard': How a Haunting Album Helped Save the Whales," written by Tim Lewis for the *Guardian* on December 6, 2020.

Florida's SaltWater Brewery is the creator of the edible six-pack rings.

Here is my arithmetic for six-pack ring to whale ratio: 6.3 billion gal. beer ÷ 2 = 3,150,000,000 gal. × 128 oz./gal. = 403,200,000,000 oz. ÷ 72 oz. (six 12 oz. beers) = 5,600,000,000 six packs × ≈ 7 in. = 39,200,000,000 in. ÷ 12 in./ft. = 3,266,666,666 ft. ÷ 39 ft. = 83,760,683 school buses, or ÷ 50 = 65,333,333 humpback whales.

Information about the advent and acceptance of the plastic bag comes from three sources: Lisa Belkin's article "Battle of the Grocery Bags:

Plastic versus Paper" in the *New York Times,* November 17, 1984; John Roach's "Planet or Plastic?" in *National Geographic,* September 2, 2003; and Sarah Laskow's "How the Plastic Bag Became So Popular" in *The Atlantic,* October 10, 2014.

The character Susan Robinson on *Sesame Street* was played by Loretta Mae Long. Her television husband, Gordon Robinson, was a high school science teacher.

News about Kenya's anti–plastic bag law appeared in the *Guardian*'s "Kenya Brings in World's Toughest Plastic Bag Ban: Four Years Jail or $40,000 Fine" on August 28, 2017.

I found the recommended lifespan of a school bus (fifteen years/250,000 miles) in a report titled "School Bus Replacement Considerations" from the National Association of State Directors of Pupil Transportation Services, published in January 2002.

The number of cars kept off the roads by each school bus came from a factsheet on the website of the American School Bus Council titled "Fact: You Can Go Green by Riding Yellow." The number thirty-six is for a fifty-four-passenger bus, though, not my standard seventy-two-passenger bus.

The ocean ecosystem dessert recipe calls for two 6 oz. boxes of blue gelatin dessert, red licorice twists, gummy fish, scissors, mint leaves, hot water, cold water, a measuring cup, a spoon, and one large, clear bowl.

The bus-sized asteroid was 2017 BX.

I use 32.5 US tons as the average humpback whale weight in my calculations, though sources vary a bit on what the maximum weight can be. The number of tons of diapers (4,100,000 tons) thrown away by Americans, the number of pounds of garbage per American per year (1,788 pounds), and the total amount of garbage a year for the United States (292.4 million US tons) came from the EPA's data for municipal solid waste generated for 2018.

The information on school bus emissions appeared in the EPA Office of Transportation and Air Quality document "Average In-Use Emissions from Urban Buses and School Buses."

THE GALÁPAGOS SHOOTING GALLERY

Information about Rollo Beck's life and early expeditions for Walter Rothschild can be found in the *Proceedings of the California Academy of Sciences* September 15, 2010, article "Collecting Galapagos and the Pacific: How Rollo Howard Beck Shaped Our Understanding of Evolution," by John P. Dumbacher and Barbara West. Rothschild's collection and museum operates still as the Natural History Museum at Tring.

All of the material from Joseph Slevin's notes comes from *Race with Extinction: Herpetological Notes of J. R. Slevin's Journey to the Galapagos 1905–1906,* edited by Thomas H. Fritts and Patricia R. Fritts.

You can read more about the philosophy of salvage collection in the chapter "Before It's Too Late" in *Collecting Evolution: The Galapagos Expedition That Vindicated Darwin,* by Matthew J. James.

The detail about Beck's collection of the last tortoise on Fernandina appears in Roger Lewin's article "Gentle Giants of the Galapagos," published in the August 3, 1978, issue of *New Scientist.* In 2019 a female tortoise was found on Fernandina, and a 2022 scientific paper in *Communications Biology* confirms that she is from the same genetic line as Beck's collected tortoise, which means that miraculously the species is not (yet) extinct.

I found the number of tortoises collected by the expedition in "Expedition of the California Academy of Sciences to the Galapagos Islands, 1906–1905," a report written by John Van Denburgh and published by the academy in 1907. While over three hundred were collected in total, the proceedings say that around forty were "more or less fragmentary remains."

I'd heard the story about Robert Capa many times but never knew the details. When I looked into it, I found that at least one photography scholar, A. D. Coleman, believes the darkroom story is a myth. You can read about his intriguing investigation in "Debunking the Myths of Robert Capa on D-Day," published in *PetaPixel* on February 16, 2019. Coleman's updates and revisions from June and July 2019 appear on his blog, *Photocritic International.*

CAGE

Many military enthusiast websites discuss the Sparrow Air Intercept Missile and its shortcomings in the Vietnam War, including Weapon-Systems.net, F-16.net, and Military-Today.com. The sites use a lot of jargon I don't understand.

Joseph Kittinger held his skydiving record for over five decades. It was broken in 2014 by Felix Baumgartner.

The quotes from Frank E. Walton about Côn Sơn came from the July 17, 1970, issue of *LIFE,* which is also where the photos were published.

My US incarceration data came from World Population Review. The Death Penalty Information Center provides detailed statistics about the number of prisoners executed in the United States. I came across a range of figures from forty-five thousand to sixty thousand for the number of juveniles detained on any day. The lower number is from the *New York Times* article "'Pacing and Praying': Jailed Youths Seek Release as Virus Spreads" by Erica L. Green, last updated October 13, 2021.

Kittinger's March 1, 1972, victory over the MiG using Sparrow missiles and his later capture are documented in *The United States Air Force in Southeast Asia: Aces and Aerial Victories 1965–1973,* edited by James N. Eastman Jr., Walter Hanak, and Lawrence J. Paszek and published by the Air Force Historical Research Agency.

The French reporter who recorded John McCain at the hospital in Hà Nội was François Chalais.

The video shown at Hòa Lò museum can be found on YouTube: "Hoa Lo Prison (Hanoi Hilton): Vietnam War POW Propaganda Piece."

I found the various meanings of "ba" in the *Vietnamese-English and English-Vietnamese Dictionary* published by Frederick Ungar Publishing Company, which I apparently borrowed quite a few years ago from our friend, writer and Vietnam War veteran Peter Scott, because his name is on the inside cover.

McCain's first-person account of his time in prison was printed in the May 14, 1973, issue of *U.S. News and World Report.*

The effect of the ritual release of birds has been covered in a number of places, including in the article "Buddhist Ceremonial Release of Captive Birds May Harm Wildlife" by Rachel Nuwer, published in *Scientific American* on August 1, 2012.

The information about notes being tossed over the wall of the Hòa Lò prison appears in Peter Zinoman's *The Colonial Bastille: A History of Imprisonment in Vietnam, 1862–1940.*

ZOO WORLD

You can buy ten twenty-gram tubes of Cobratoxan for fifty-five dollars. Each contains 0.0005 grams of cobra venom.

Because of questions of legitimacy of the 1989 name change by the government, different publications and nations take different approaches to what name they use for the country of Myanmar or Burma. Some entities simply use both. While traveling in the country in 2014, I heard both. I've chosen to use "Myanmar" to refer to the current nation, as that has become widely acceptable, though the US government still uses "Burma."

I found conflicting stories about the last king of Burma, King Thibaw, and his white elephant. Some said that when his elephant died, the country fell under British rule, and some that the white elephant eventually on display at the zoo in 1906 belonged to him. Which is true? Jonathan Saha writes about the king and his white elephant both on his blog *Colonizing Animals* and in his book of the same name. He concludes that there may have been two white elephants.

News about Thailand's request to borrow a white elephant in June 2013 and Myanmar's response was reported in a number of publications, including the *Nation Thailand* and *Bangkok Post*. Myanmar's response was that they could arrange special flights for visitors from Chiang Mai (where Thai officials wanted to display the elephant) to come see the elephants in Yangon instead.

The story about the giraffes in the West Bank zoo appeared on March 5, 2003, in the *New York Times* article "Qalqiliya Journal: In a Man-Ravaged Bank, A Petrified Zoo," by James Bennet. The Giza Zoo details appeared in a December 19, 2013, article in the *Independent*, "'Hell for Animals': Egypt's Giza Zoo Beset by Tear Gas, Bear 'Riots' and Giraffe 'suicide,'" by Abigail Hauslohner. Information about of the graves at the Nashville Zoo was reported in 2014 by Michael Cass in several articles in the *Tennessean*. The details about dismemberment of the Danish giraffe appeared many places, including in *CBS News* on February 11, 2014, which included photos. Frederik Pleitgen reported the Gaza Zoo story, including information about the reporters bringing chickens, for *CNN* on August 22, 2014, in "Gaza's Zoo Animals Caught in Crossfire of Israel-Hamas Conflict." I read the Bangkok crocodile story "Suicide by Crocodile Pit: Elderly Woman Torn Apart by Dozens of the Giant Reptiles after Jumping into Pond at Zoo," by Simon Tomlinson, on the *Daily-Mail* online, published September 16, 2014. The BBC News reported the white tiger incident on September 23, 2014, in "Indian White Tiger Kills Man at Delhi Zoo." Neil MacFarquhar reported "Zoo Animals on the Loose in Tbilisi after Flooding" for the *New York Times* on June 14, 2015.

I read about the downed B-52 in the Hà Nội Zoological Park in the article "The Modest Victors" by Harish Chandola, published in the March 10, 1973, issue of *Economic and Political Weekly*.

The Ohio Department of Natural Resources website confirms the squirrel-as-taxes story but also mentions the 1885 hunting laws.

Rusty's escape from the zoo was covered by major news outlets everywhere. Read about the coverage of his escape in Trip Gabriel's *New York Times* piece "A Panda Escapes from the Zoo and Social Media Swoop In with the Net" from June 24, 2013.

The Smithsonian National Zoological Park website posted about Buzz's death at the time. The post called him a "laid-back, calm beaver" and said he was fourteen years old, "geriatric for a beaver."

Since I wrote this essay, zoos in distress continue to make the news, including the Kyiv Zoo in 2022. You can read about zookeepers moving into the zoo with their families to take care of the animals in Siobhán O'Grady and Kostiantyn Khudov's article "A Blast-Stressed Elephant and an Abandoned Lemur: The War within Kyiv's Zoo," which appeared in the *Washington Post* on March 6, 2022.

IN THE CLASSROOM

Resources for this essay include Peter Maguire's *Facing Death in Cam-*

bodia, Elizabeth Becker's *When the War Was Over: Cambodia and the Khmer Rouge Revolution,* David P. Chandler's *Voices from S-21: Terror and History in Pol Pot's Secret Prison* and *A History of Cambodia,* and Meng-Try Ea and Sorya Sim's *Victims or Perpetrator? Testimony of Young Khmer Rouge Comrades,* published by the Documentation Center of Cambodia, which has archived thousands of pages of records, photographs, and interviews in the name of memory and justice.

A report titled *An Honor and an Ornament: Public School Buildings in Michigan* published by the State Historic Preservation Office, Michigan Historical Center, and the Michigan Department of History, Arts and Libraries mentions the beliefs of twentieth-century school designers regarding light and eye strain, though it doesn't explain why they thought this was true.

William C. Adams and Michael Joblove's chapter titled "The Unnewsworthy Holocaust: TV News and Terror in Cambodia" in *Television Coverage of International Affairs,* edited by William C. Adams, provides the number of minutes of television news coverage of the genocide from 1975–78.

The percentage of secondary teachers killed appears in *Cambodia: A Country Study,* edited by Russell R. Ross and published by the Library of Congress.

In the years since I first wrote about the Khmer Rouge Tribunal, three other Khmer Rouge defendants have been charged by the Extraordinary Chambers in the Courts of Cambodia (ECCC) but not convicted: Meas Muth, Yim Tith, and Ao An. A fourth, Sou Met, died before he could be charged. Charges were dismissed against Im Chaem in 2020.

The case against Ao An was terminated in 2020. The website for the ECCC is vast and full of legal documents as well as information for victims of the Khmer Rouge.

Also in the time since this essay was written, more schools have suffered horrific shootings. Parents and students at Marjory Stoneman Douglas High School, where seventeen people were killed in 2018, have asked that the building where the shootings took place be razed. According to Joan Murray's October 19, 2022, article for *CBS News Miami,* "Target Date Set for Return of MSD Belongings Frozen in Time at Crime Scene," the building will likely be demolished in 2023 after the last trial associated with the shooting is complete and the belongings that have been sitting in the classrooms for years are finally returned. Robb Elementary School, where twenty-one people were killed in 2022, will be demolished.

In 2023 Chum Mey, in his early nineties, is the last living survivor of S-21.

PARADISE, EARTH

The main sources I reference are *The Last Emperors of Vietnam: From Tu Duc to Bao Dai,* by Oscar Chapuis; *Understanding Vietnam,* by Neil L. Jamieson; *A Story of Việt Nam,* by Truong Buu Lâm; *The Vietnamese Response to French Intervention, 1862–1874,* by Mark W. McLeod; *The History of Vietnam,* by Justin Corfield; *Vietnam: A History,* by Stanley Karnow; and *The Rough Guide to Vietnam* (sixth edition), by Jan Dodd, Ron Emmons, Mark Lewis, and Martin Zatko. Many of the more vivid details attached to Tự Đức's life and family come from Chapuis, who used as his sources work by scholars Trịnh Văn Thanh (*Thành ngữ điển tích danh nhân từ điển*), Trần Trọng Kim (*Việt Nam sử lược*), and Phạm Văn Sơn (*Việt sử tân biên*). Other sources include various tourist and travel websites who themselves use sources as unknown as the afterlife.

I read Nguyễn Công Trứ's poem "A Wasted Life" in *An Anthology of Vietnamese Poems: From the Eleventh through the Twentieth Centuries,* edited and translated by Huỳnh Sanh Thông. The full poem is:

> Thirty-thousand days—the human span.
> Some sixteen thousand I've already spent.
> I'll ask the Maker, "Please turn time around
> And give a man more scope wherein to play!"

FONOTECA NACIONAL

A previous owner of Casa Alvarado, American archeologist Zelia Nuttall, was apparently responsible for promoting the story that Pedro de Alvarado had lived on the property. Her friend Philip Ainsworth Means composed an affectionate tribute to her in the *Hispanic American Historical Review* shortly after her death in 1933, calling her "one of the outstanding figures in American archeology and history during a full half century" and also a "truly rare personality." He reports that she got into a lot of arguments with other scholars. ("Many a cocksure person who differed with her on scientific questions received a sound drubbing for his pains, her weapons being the bludgeon of authentic fact and the rapier of valid argument.") Still, while saying (somewhat defensively) that "is it likely that Casa Alvarado *is* the oldest mansion in the new world," he also acknowledges that this story may or may not be true. In the end he seems under the impression that the house will become a national monument and suggests that it should be a memorial to Nuttall. It isn't. The Mexican sources I found all agreed the story of Alvarado is fiction.

The 2001 articles describing the house as "somewhat crumbling" and "dark, crumbling" were from the *Washington Post* (Mary Jordan's "In Mexico, Bitter Words over a Writer's Legacy," published January 18, 2001) and the *Los Angeles Times* (Jill Leovy's "Mexican Scholars Lament the Loss of Writers' Archives to U.S.," published February 25, 2001).

I learned about the story of Paz's estate, archive, and the DIF through numerous articles published in *El Universal, Excelsior,* and *Milenio* as the situation unfolded in 2021. The bulletin for Instituto Nacional de Bellas Artes y Literatura also provided me with details about the fate of the Paz archive.

My understanding of Marie-José Tramini developed from the portrait created of her by writer and environmental activist Homero Aridjis in his essay "On Octavio Paz and Marie-José Tramini," which appeared in the November 2019 issue of the *London Review of Books,* her portrayal in the article by Mary Jordan mentioned above, and Stephanie Nolen's reporting in "A Mexican Poet's Muse Dies—and Throws His Legacy into Turmoil," published in the *Globe and Mail* on March 2, 2019.

I drew information about the physical state of Paz's archive and the many cats from Homero Aridjis as well as from Alida Piñón's article "El archivo de Paz ya está en proceso de catalogación," published in *El Universal* on August 24, 2019.

GALL

Alfred Kinsey's gall wasp studies are cited in the article "Review of the World Genera of Oak Cynipid Wasps" by George Melika and Warren G. Abrahamson, where I first read about *Acraspis erinacei*.

IN HARMONY WITH NATURE

The study "Indifference to Dissonance in Native Amazonians Reveals Cultural Variation in Music Perception," by Josh H. McDermott, Alan F. Schultz, Eduardo A. Undurraga, and Ricardo A. Godoy, appeared in *Nature*, volume 535, issue 7613.

Cleveland *Plain Dealer* reporter James F. McCarty wrote about Aqua-Salina as deicer in the article "Radioactive Road Deicer Rules under Review by Ohio Legislature: Debate over Public Safety Continues," published February 10, 2019.

I read about vaccines that may help with methane reduction in the BBC article "The Cows That Could Help Fight Climate Change" by Geoff Watts, published August 6, 2019. The study about breeding less methaney cows, "A Heritable Subset of the Core Rumen Microbiome Dictates Dairy Cow Productivity and Emissions," appeared in volume 5, issue 7, of *Science Advances* on July 3, 2019, and involved thirty-some scientists and a thousand cows across Europe.

As someone who's grown a lot of tomatoes, I'm well acquainted with braconid wasps. If you want to read more, check out an insect guide, such as the Ohio Division of Wildlife's *Common Bees and Wasps of Ohio* field guide.

Information about the state of Wisconsin dairy farms is from articles by *Milwaukee Journal Sentinel* and *USA TODAY NETWORK-Wisconsin* journalists in 2019 as part of a fascinating series called Dairyland in Distress. I highly recommend it to all milk-carton readers.

The number of dairy cows in the United States appeared in the July 24, 2019, United Press International (UPI) article "U.S. Loses 100,000 Dairy Cows in Last Year as More Dairy Farms Close," by Jessie Higgins. The milk glut was covered in Dairyland in Distress and also in "'Too Much Milk': Production Is Up, Prices Are Down and Farmers Are in Crisis" by Steven Elbow in the *Cap Times,* February 27, 2019. I read about the effect of the coronavirus pandemic on dairies in several places, including the article "Milk Scarce at Some Grocery Stores, but Dairy Glut Has Farmers Dumping It Down the Drain" by Associated Press journalist Lisa Rathke, which appeared in the *Chicago Tribune* on April 14, 2020. News about cows being slaughtered also appeared in a number of places, such as the May 8, 2020, *TIME* article "Dairy Cows Are Being Sent to Slaughter as Demand for Milk Plummets," by Jen Skerritt and Michael Hirtzer.

I read about CAFOs in the National Association of Local Boards of Health 2010 publication *Understanding Concentrated Animal Feeding Operations and Their Impact on Communities,* by Carrie Hribar. The percentage of milk produced by large CAFOs comes from the USDA's 2017 Census of Agriculture report on dairy cattle and milk production. The *Washington Post* story "Why Your 'Organic' Milk May Not Be Organic," by Peter Whoriskey, appeared May 1, 2017.

Cow shit math: a 1,400-pound Holstein produces 115 pounds of manure a day according to the 1998 study "Energy Aspects of Manure Management," authored by David B. Fischer for the University of Illinois Extension.

I learned about the impact of frac sand mines on communities in "How Fracking's Appetite for Sand Is Devouring Rural Communities" by anthropologist Thomas W. Pearson, published in *SAPIENS* on May 4, 2018. The percentage of frac sand mines that could close was reported by Wisconsin Public Radio news in "Frac Sand Producer in Wisconsin Faces Bankruptcy as Industry Shifts" by Rich Kremer, published May 13, 2019.

STEEL

All of the details of the scenarios with our hero are taken from *Action Comics* nos. 1, 5, 6, 8, 9, 10, 11, 12, and 13, released June 1938–June 1939, and the limited-edition *New York World's Fair Comics* no. 1, released in April 1939.

I didn't identify those involved, but if you are left wondering, here they are. The famous safety director is Eliot Ness, and the murders he's investigating are known as the Torso Murders. The serial killer at the duplex is Anthony Sowell. The young artists are Jerry Siegel and Joe Shuster. The hero is Kal-El.

the journal non/fiction prize
(formerly the ohio state university prize in short fiction)

Printed in the USA
CPSIA information can be obtained
at www.ICGtesting.com
LVHW041807050124
767856LV00001B/38

9 780814 258774